Blossom by blossom the spring begins...

Beautiful Banners
More Than 70 Festive Designs To Decorate Your Home

Beautiful Banners

More Than 70 Festive Designs To Decorate Your Home

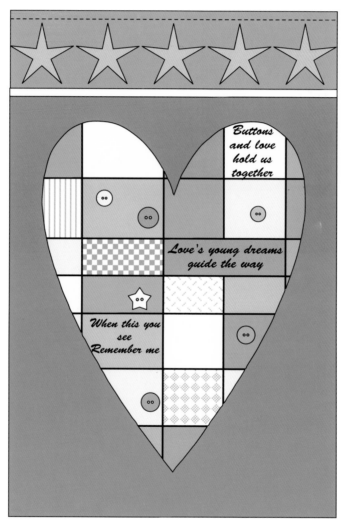

Buttons and love hold us together

Love's young dreams guide the way

When this you see Remember me

Barbara Webster

Sterling Publishing Co., Inc. New York

A Sterling/Chapelle Book

For Chapelle Ltd.

Owner
Jo Packham
Editor
Cherie Hanson

Staff
Malissa Boatwright • Sara Casperson • Rebecca Christensen
Holly Fuller • Amber Hansen • Holly Hollingsworth
Susan Jorgensen • Susan Laws • Amanda McPeck
Barbara Milburn • Pat Pearson • Leslie Ridenour
Cindy Rooks • Cindy Stoeckl • Ryanne Webster • Nancy Whitley
Designers
Amber Fuller • Holly Fuller • Sharon Ganske • Roberta Glidden
Mary Jo Hiney • Gloria Judson • Susan Laws • Barbara Milburn
Jo Packham • Jamie Pierce • Phillip Romero • Cindy Rooks
Photography
Kevin Dilley for Hazen Photography
Styling
Susan Laws

If you have any questions or comments or would like information on specialty products featured in this book, please contact:
Chapelle, Ltd., Inc., PO Box 9252, Ogden, UT 84409
801-621-2777 (phone), 801-621-2788 (fax).

The written instructions, photographs, designs, patterns and projects in this volume are intended for the personal use of the reader and may be reproduced for that purpose only. Any other use, especially commercial use, is forbidden under law without the written permission of the copyright holder.

Every effort has been made to ensure that all the information in this book is accurate. However, due to differing conditions, tools, and individual skills, the publisher cannot be responsible for any injuries, losses, and other damages which may result from the use of the information in this book.

Graduation Banner pattern on page 116.

Library of Congress Cataloging-in Publication Data

Webster, Barbara. 1958–
    Beautiful banners :   more than 70 festive designs to decorate your home / by Barbara Webster.
        p.   cm.
"A Sterling/Chapelle book."
Includes index.
ISBN 0-8069-4862-0
    1. Flags. 2. Wall hangings. I. Title.
TT850.2.W43   1996
746. 3—dc20   96-4993
                                                              CIP

3 5 7 9 10 8 6 4 2
Published by Sterling Publishing Company, Inc.
387 Park Avenue South, New York, N.Y. 10016
© 1996 by Chapelle Ltd.
Distributed in Canada by Sterling Publishing
℅ Canadian Manda Group, One Atlantic Avenue, Suite 105
Toronto, Ontario, Canada M6K 3E7
Distributed in Great Britain and Europe by Cassell PLC
Wellington House, 125 Strand, London WC2R 0BB, England
Distributed in Australia by Capricorn Link (Australia) Pty Ltd.
P.O. Box 6651, Baulkham Hills, Business Center, NSW 2153, Australia
Printed in Hong Kong
All rights reserved

Sterling ISBN 0-8069-4862-0

Contents

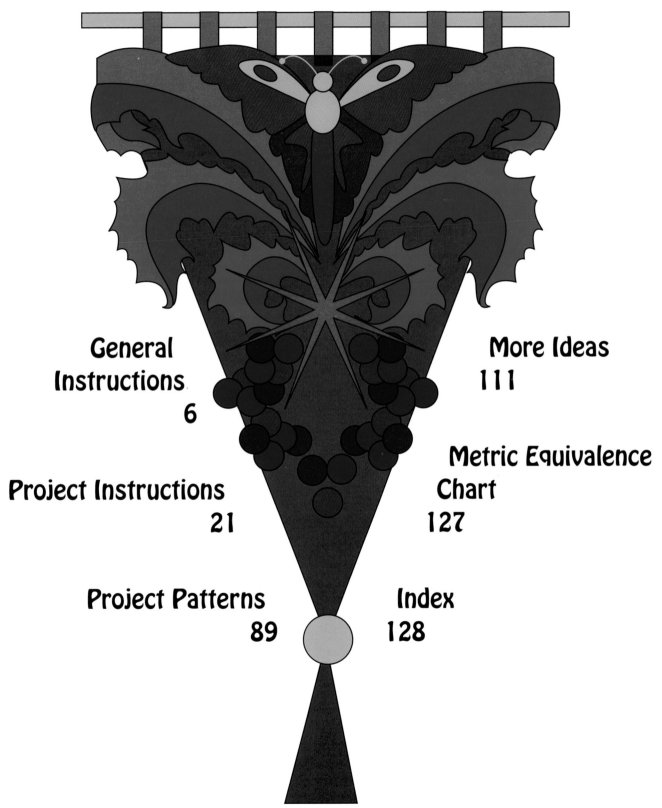

General Instructions

Terms

Appliqué: The art of applying fabric cutouts or other materials to a background in order to create a decorative pattern.

Basting: Stitches used to hold motifs in place on the background until secured by some means.

Double-Sided Fusible Web: Often used to secure a motif to a background before stitching. A web with weak adhesive can easily be removed if desired. Different webs are made for different types of fabric.

Finial: A crowning ornament added to the end of a dowel or rod.

Fused Appliqué (Bonded Appliqué): Use of fusible fabric adhesive or iron-on interfacing to bond the design to the background.

Grommet: An eyelet of firm material, such as metal, used to strengthen the hole on the banner to hang it from. Use a grommet tool to attach grommets to banners.

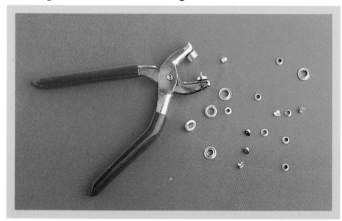

Hand-Stitched Appliqué: Hand-stitching fabric cutouts to a background.

Iron-on Interfacing: Used to stiffen loosely woven fabrics and knits, to prevent a dark background from showing through a light foreground, or to make frayable fabrics more manageable. Creates a crisp look. Different weights are made for different types of fabric.

Machine-Stitched Appliqué: Machine-stitching fabric cutouts to a background. Good for heavy fabrics that are difficult to hand-stitch or for items that will be used heavily or laundered frequently. Has a sharper appearance than hand-stitched appliqué.

Mixed-Media Appliqué: Use of other materials in combination with fabric to create a design. Can also refer to the use of dying and hand-painting techniques in combination with appliqué or the use of several appliqué techniques.

Motif: A piece of the appliqué design.

Padded Appliqué (3/D Appliqué): Use of some type of padding to make the appliqué more dimensional.

Rip-Away Backing: A lightweight paper or tissue used to add stability to fabrics and keep them from puckering or stretching while sewing.

Shadow Appliqué: Placing solid-colored fabrics on a background, then covering those fabrics with sheer fabric to create a shadow effect.

Template: A reference drawing of the desired finished appliqué. It is also used to make patterns.

Tracing Paper: Drawing paper that has a transparent characteristic. Place paper over patterns and transfer the lines that are visible through the tracing paper.

Transfer Paper: Often called dressmaker's carbon. It is a paper that is coated on one side used to transfer designs onto fabrics or other materials.

Turned-Edge Appliqué (Blind Appliqué): The edges of the cutout fabric turned under or hemmed before or during appliquéing them to the background. There is no visible stitching around the design in this method.

Fabrics & Threads For Banners

All kinds of fabrics can be used for the projects in this book—plain, patterned, smooth, textured, thick and thin. The type and style of fabric used depends on the desired look of the finished product and the skill of the crafter. Cotton fabrics are the most common, and are among the easiest to use. Unwoven fabrics, like felt and leathers, are particularly easy to cut and handle and can be used by both beginner and expert alike. Other fabrics, like silks and satins, require skill and care to use but add sophistication to a piece.

The type of fabric should match the style of the piece. For example, a bright-colored felt would be just right for use in a child's banner but inappropriate for a Victorian piece.

It is also important to take into account the scale of any patterns printed on fabric. Small motifs can be very versatile and will work well even in a small piece. Larger motifs have a limited number of uses and cannot be seen if the cutout is small.

Also keep in mind how easily a fabric frays. A fabric that frays very easily may be hard to work with, and the edges will have to be secured in some way.

The following are different types of fabric used for projects in this book:

Rip-Stop Nylon: Perfect for outdoor banners, is machine washable, easy to work with, lightweight yet durable, and comes in a wide range of colors. Be sure to purchase nylon with a UV protective coating to resist fading.

Canvas: Heavyweight woven fabric. Provides a stable backing.

Cotton/Polyester Blends: Common fabric for banners. Lightweight and washable. Comes in a wide variety of colors and prints.

Ultra Suede (artificial): Non-woven material that is ideal for banners using the no-sew technique. This fabric is lighter than genuine ultra suede. Use mainly on indoor banners that do not need cleaning.

Felt: A good choice for indoor banners that are never laundered or dry-cleaned. Also works well using the no-sew technique. Use wool or polyester felt, never acrylic or craft felt.

Silk: Excellent for indoor banners. Creates a formal look. May need extra stabilization with a backing fabric, padding, or interfacing.

Thread Choice: The same considerations for fabric choice also apply to thread choice. The type of thread used should be appropriate for the use and style of the finished piece. Sometimes contrasting stitching adds as much to the design as the material itself.

Another consideration in choosing threads is the type of fabric used. Like threads should go with like fabrics. Natural threads should be used with natural fabrics and synthetic threads with synthetic fabrics.

Preparing Fabric: All fabrics should be clean and pressed (if possible) before using. Make certain the fabric used is preshrunk and colorfast if the finished piece will be washed or hung outdoors. Also check to make certain the grain line is straight by pulling out a weft thread near the edge of the fabric and cutting along the gap.

Backing Fabric: A backing fabric is used as a support for fabrics that need extra firmness and strength. Most lightweight and stretch fabrics need a backing fabric as do banners that need to support weighted embellishments. The backing fabric should be pre-washed and correspond in weight to the fabric it is applied to. Cut the backing fabric larger than the finished design of the appliqué to allow for seams, finishing, and/or mounting. Iron-on interfacing can also be used to give body and strength to a thin fabric.

Transferring the Design

The first step in making any banner is to make a template or full-scale outlined drawing of the design. This full-scale template will be used to mark the background, to make patterns for the motifs, and as a reference during the construction of the piece.

1. On 1" dressmaker's grid paper, mark dots on grid where the pattern in the book intersects its corresponding grid line. When all dots have been marked, connect the dots to finish pattern. Note: Instead of purchasing dressmaker's grid paper, make grid paper by drawing horizontal and vertical lines, spaced 1" apart on paper large enough to accommodate the pattern at actual size.

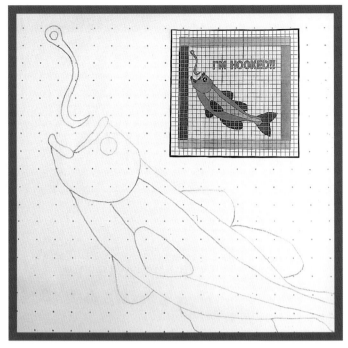

2. Transfer the design onto the background fabric using one of the following techniques.

Window or Light Table: The simplest means of marking the design on the background is tracing using a light table or a bright window. Of course this method only works if the background is lightweight and/or light colored.

Transfer Paper: Another means of marking the design on the background is to use transfer paper, or sometimes called dressmaker's carbon. Do not use office carbon paper as it will leave permanent marks. Since transfer paper comes in many colors choose a paper that is closest in color and tone to the background fabric but will still be visible. Be certain to follow the manufacturer's directions.

Patterns and Chalk: Another way to transfer the design is to make cardboard or paper patterns and use dressmaker's chalk, fabric markers, or a soft pencil to mark the design. This method is not quite as accurate as the first two and it is harder to mark the placement of motifs if they are not a part of the outer edge of the design.

Tracing Paper: Tracing paper can also be used to mark the outline. Pin the tracing paper to the background fabric then pin or baste along the lines. Tear the paper away. This method is also not as accurate as tracing the design directly onto the fabric or using transfer paper.

Making Patterns For Appliqué

The tracing or the transfer paper methods can be used to transfer the design on the motif fabrics as well as the background. If neither method is feasible, patterns must be made for the motifs to ensure they are cut precisely. The pattern can be made from a variety of materials. X-ray film, stencil plastic, or thick tracing paper are all good choices because they are semitransparent.

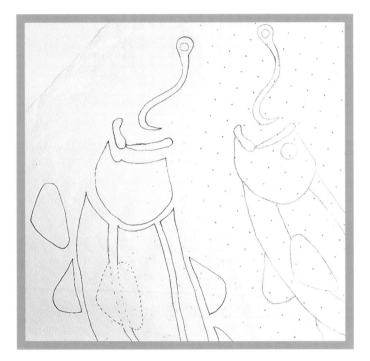

1. Trace each piece of the design from the full-scale template onto tracing paper. Mark the grain lines on each piece of the design. Cut out each pattern piece. The pattern can then be transferred to a thicker material if desired.

2. Pin the pattern to the fabric and cut out. Cut on a flat surface so that the fabric does not pucker or draw. Be certain to add seam allowances if necessary. If using a thicker pattern, place the pattern on the fabric, pin in place, and mark the design with dressmaker's chalk, fabric markers, or a soft pencil. If using fabric with a pile, it is easier to transfer the design to the back of the fabric, making certain to transfer a mirror image of the design.

Assembling Appliqué: Place the motifs over the marked outlines on the background fabric. If another means has been used, the motifs can be positioned by eye, using the full-scale template for positioning.

Note: Plan the construction of the piece carefully. Sometimes it is easier to overlap pieces than to fit them together exactly. Be careful when overlapping a light fabric over a dark one, as the bottom, darker fabric may show through.

Keeping Fabric Flat: When doing machine appliqué, rip-away backing is often used to hold fabric in place and prevent tiny puckers in the fabric. It is placed on the bottom layer of the fabric to be stitched. When the stitching is complete, the paper is torn off. If no rip-away backing is available, thick tissue paper or typing paper can be used.

When doing hand appliqué, good basting is essential. A motif should be basted in place with stitches running both directions to prevent the fabric from puckering. First, find the center of the fabric, then baste from the center in each direction toward the outside. Additional basting may be needed, but be certain to always start from the center to prevent any puckering of the fabric.

An embroidery hoop can be used to further hold fabric taut. If the area to be appliquéd is too large for an embroidery hoop, a frame can be used to pull fabric taut.

Changing a Design: The colors in the diagrams in this book are only suggestions. Remember that a design can look completely different by changing the colors or techniques. In some instances, different color schemes of the same banner have been included. Also remember that the pattern and texture of the fabric or paints used in a design will make it look different as well. Feel free to change colors, patterns, and textures as desired. For a simple project transfer the patterns onto the backing fabric and paint in the desired designs. For a more difficult project, appliqué the entire banner. An intermediate project would be a combination of painting and appliqué. Decide which techniques work the best and adapt them to any project.

The designs in this book can also be easily mixed and matched to create new designs. Motifs from one design will often work well with motifs from another. Keep in mind that if a banner is to be viewed from both sides, such as outdoor banners, two banners should be made and stitched together back to back.

Finding the Center: Most designs may be positioned simply by eye, but some need more precision. To find the center of the design fold the paper pattern into quarters and mark two pencil lines along the folds. To check if the exact center has been located draw a diagonal line from corner to corner. If it intersects the middle of the

crossed horizontal and vertical lines you have found the exact center of the design.

The center of the fabric can be found in a similar manner. Fold the fabric in quarters and mark the lines with basting stitches. When transferring the design to the fabric use the pencil and basting lines to check the alignment.

Methods of Appliqué

The following pages contain step-by-step instructions for several different methods of appliqué. Keep in mind that appliqué techniques are often used together and one project can incorporate several methods of appliqué. The quickest method of appliqué is to combine the fused method with the machine-stitched, fusing the motifs to a background and then machine-stitching over the edges.

The more work done by hand and the more complicated the method used, the more time-consuming a project will be. A two-hour machine-stitched project would be a day's work done with hand-stitching.

Some methods of appliqué are more appropriate for certain designs than others. Choose an appliqué method that fits both the chosen design and desired finished product.

This Congratulations banner pattern is on page 113.

Hand-Stitched Appliqué

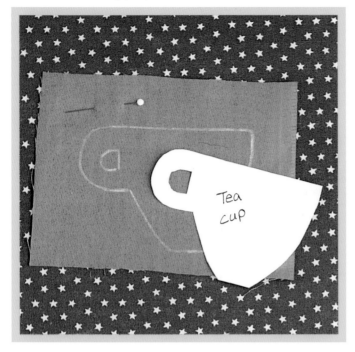

1. Place pattern right side down on wrong side of fabric. Trace and cut out shape. Label.

2. If fabric frays easily, secure edges with a fray preventative or secure using matching thread and stitching overcast stitches, backstitches, or running stitches.

3. Pin motif in appropriate place on marked background. Baste.

4. Stitch over edges with desired decorative stitch to conceal securing stitches. If edges do not fray, motif can be secured with stab stitching. Remove basting stitches.

Turned-Edge Appliqué (Blind Appliqué)

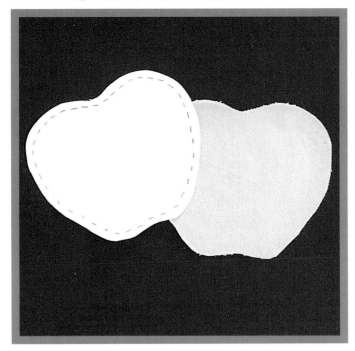

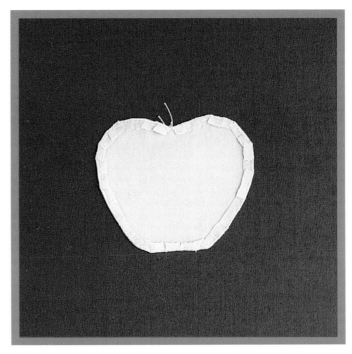

1. Trace and cut out motif, leaving a ¹/₈" to ¹/₂" seam allowance. Lighter-weight fabrics need a larger seam allowance than heavier-weight fabrics. Machine-straight-stitch along actual motif line, or cut out iron-on interfacing to actual motif size and iron onto motif fabric.

2. Fold seam allowance to wrong side, using stitching or interfacing as a guide. Snip, notch, or trim allowance as needed. Baste edges in place.

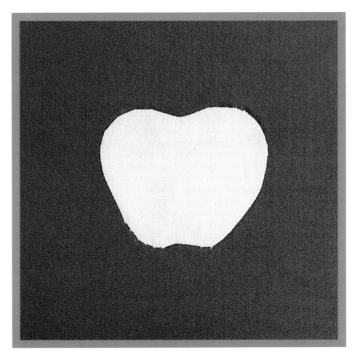

3. Iron for a crisp, flat edge, or leave unpressed for a slight relief.

4. Pin prepared motif in place on marked background; baste. Secure with chosen stitch. Remove basting stitches.

Machine-Stitched Appliqué

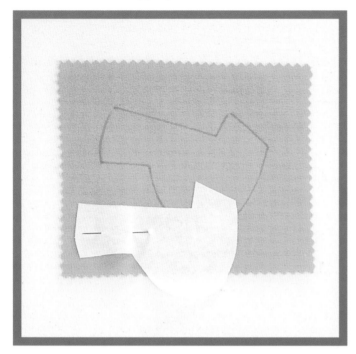

1. Trace motif pattern onto fabric. Cut fabric a little larger than actual design. Place motif on marked background. Baste onto background fabric to minimize puckering.

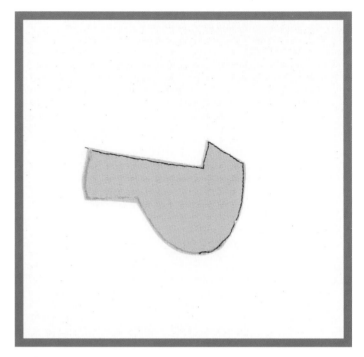

2. Sew over exact traced line on motif with straight stitches. Trim away extra fabric.

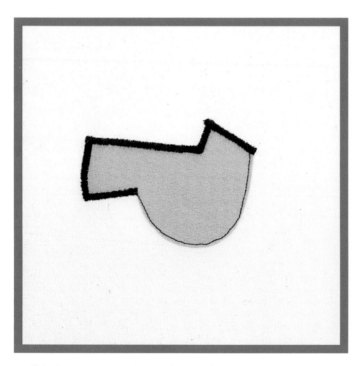

3. Stitch over raw edges with a short, close zig zag or satin stitch.

4. Trim away all visible basting threads. Press to ease out any small wrinkles. Snip off raw edges and bits of thread with embroidery scissors.

No-Sew Appliqué

No-sew appliqué should be used on banners that do not require cleaning. In other instances, this method is used as a preparation for sewing rather than an independent method. Use this method without securing stitches only for infrequently used items.

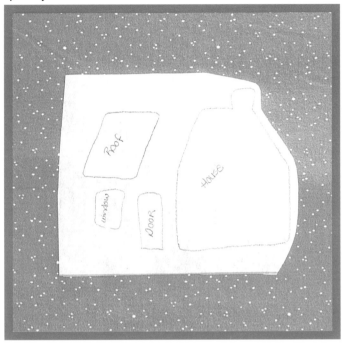

1. Trace reverse design on nonadhesive, paper-side of double-sided fusible web (outline will be a mirror image of motif). Cut out web motif, allowing a small margin.

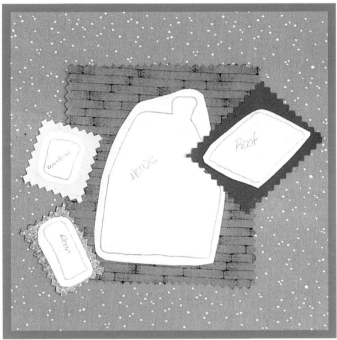

2. Iron unbacked (adhesive-side) to appliqué fabric, matching grain lines and following manufacturer's instructions. Cut out motif along exact pattern line with sharp embroidery scissors.

3. Peel away backing paper, and iron motif to marked background, following manufacturer's instructions.

4. Cover edges with machine-, hand-stitching, or paint, depending on the desired effect and amount of use.

Shadow Appliqué

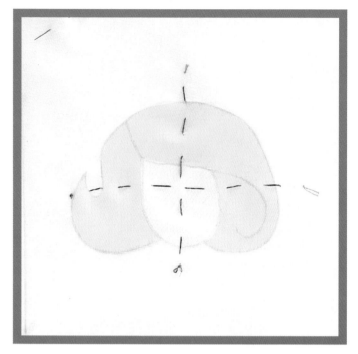

Method One: 1. Baste a sheer fabric on top of desired shadow motif matching grains. Draw design on sheer fabric and stitch over lines.

2. Cut away excess sheer fabric close to stitching line. Apply to background as desired.

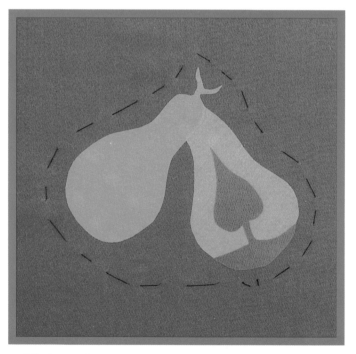

Method Two: 1. Cut motifs and secure to background as desired. Pin sheer fabric over entire design and baste around edges.

2. Work small running stitches around the edge of motifs. Cut away fabric at lines of stitching or stitch around edges of finished piece for a quilted effect.

Padded Appliqué

Felt Option: 1. Cut several pieces of felt the same shape as motif each slightly smaller than the other.

2. Starting with the smallest felt piece pin and stab-stitch to center of area to be padded. Repeat with other pieces. Sew covering fabric on top with turned-edge method.

Batting Option: Cut required batting the same size as motif and the required thickness. Stitch batting to back ground with loosely tensioned straight stitches. Stitch motif covering fabric on top of batting using turned-edge method.

Cardboard Option: Center cardboard on wrong side of motif covering fabric. Wrap edges to back and secure with fabric glue. Slip-stitch to background around edges.

Note: For all options, covering fabric must be cut slightly larger than pattern to accommodate padding.

15

Mixed Media Appliqué

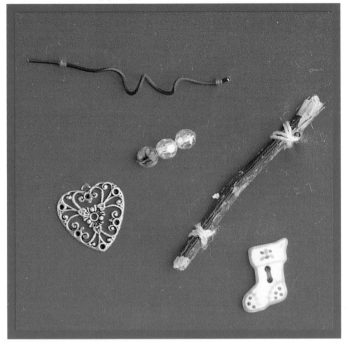

1. Buttons, beads, and sequins should be sewn on in the traditional manner.

2. Other objects like tiny mirrors or small twigs are secured with buttonhole stitching.

3. Most objects can be secured with fabric glue, tacky glue, or industrial-strength adhesive. Check to make certain the glue used will not stain fabric and will hold for desired use.

Other Sewing Methods
Hand Quilting
1. Layer finished appliquéd banner and lining fabric together with right sides facing, then layer fleece or batting on the lining side.

2. Sew around the edges, leaving a small opening in one seam. Turn through opening, slip-stitch closed.

3. Before quilting, baste through all layers to prevent shifting.

4. Hand-stitch design following quilting lines.

5. When all stitching is completed, remove basting stitches.

Machine Quilting

1. Layer finished appliquéd banner and lining fabric together with right sides facing, then layer fleece or batting on the lining side.

2. Sew around the edges, leaving a small opening in one seam. Turn through opening, slip-stitch closed.

3. Before quilting, baste through all layers to prevent shifting.

4. Cover or lower the sewing machine's feed dogs. Loosen the pressure on the presser foot. Use a darning or free-motion presser foot if available.

5. Stitch along quilting lines at a steady, even pace.

6. When all stitching is completed, remove basting stitches.

Machine Embroidering Letters
1. Trace letters onto the banner, using a removable marking pencil.

2. Place portion of banner to be embroidered in a hoop.

3. To allow enough room to insert hoop under needle, remove sewing machine foot and raise needle.

16

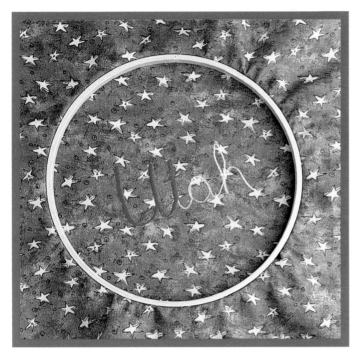

4. Cover or lower the sewing machine's feed dogs. Loosen the pressure on the presser foot. Use a darning or free-motion presser foot if available.

5. Stitch along marked lines at a steady, even pace using a satin- or straight stitch.

Hand Embroidery

Hand embroidery is the type of hand-stitch used on the projects in this book. These stitches can be used to secure motifs to background fabrics or for decorative purposes only. The following are the basic stitches used:

Blanket Stitches

Blanket stitches create a distinct pattern, are especially effective on edges, and used as a tool for outlining as well. Come up at A and go down at B. Come back up at C, allowing thread to tack itself against the fabric. Repeat to achieve desired length.

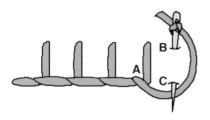

Stab Stitches

A line of straight stitches with an unstitched area between each stitch. Come up at A and go down at B. Repeat to desired length.

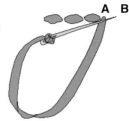

Herringbone Stitches

The herringbone stitch is a pleasing pattern for a border or design. Come up at A and go down at B, coming up at C. Go down at D, coming back up again at E. Repeat to achieve desired length.

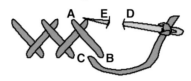

Painting

After the patterns have been traced, paint in the background colors first, then go back and paint fine details. It should be like coloring in a coloring book—just stay within the lines.

Acrylic or water-based paints work best because they dry quickly and come in a variety of pre-mixed colors. They clean up easily with soap and water when still wet. Be sure to clean your brushes thoroughly with soap and water until the water runs clear.

Oil paints are used when you may want to mix your own colors and tints. Oil paint has a translucent quality and dries slowly, which allows you to do elaborate blending and shading. Oil paints require paint thinner for clean up.

All paints need to be mixed with textile medium. Textile medium is a necessary additive that prevents paints from peeling and helps to permanently adhere them to fabrics. The ratio of medium added to the paint depends on the amount of opacity of the paint desired. The more medium added, the more transparent the color becomes. Paint project as desired with paint and medium mixture. Allow to set following manufacturer's instructions. Apply iron to the back side of painted fabric for 20 seconds, or place in clothsdryer on high for 20 minutes. Wait five days after application if banner is to be laundered.

Painting Faces and Fine Details

To paint faces and fine details, be sure surface to be painted has dried thoroughly if previously painted. Using a fine point brush appropriate for design, begin painting the larger details. Paint the smaller details, such as outlines, last.

Blending

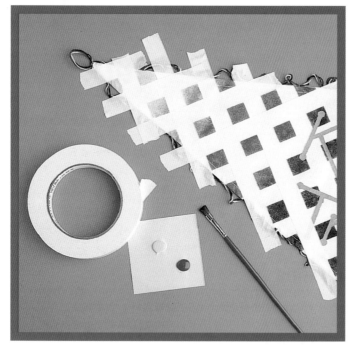

Blending is a technique in which two or more paints are mixed together directly on the surface to be painted, creating highlights and shadows. Begin by applying first color—do not let dry. Apply the second color onto the fabric overlapping the first color as desired. Gradually mix the paints together along the overlapping edges in swirling or back-and-forth strokes.

Now in a home built of flowers and laughter, I know the meaning of the words "ever after".

Flowers & Laughter Chair banner pattern is on page 121.

Stenciling

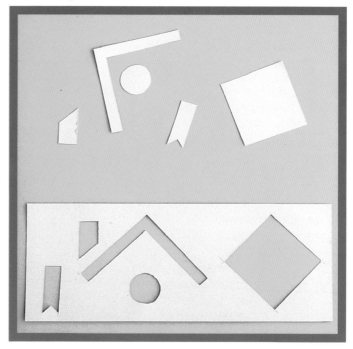

Transfer pattern onto a plastic stencil sheet– a piece of clear acetate, manila folder, posterboard, or lightweight cardboard also work well. Using a craft knife, or or single-edged razor, cut the portion of the design to be stenciled from the acetate or cardboard. Secure the stencil in place with tape on the surface to be stenciled. Load a stencil paintbrush with paint and blot excess—too much paint on the brush will seep under stencil. (This technique is called dry brushing.) Stroke from edges inward across the cut portion of the stencil. Remove stencil and fill in any unwanted gaps if desired.

To blend stenciling like on the Keep On Trikin' banner on page 61, repeat as above except use two stencil paintbrushes loaded with different colors of paint. With one paintbrush, begin stroking from the edges inward in one direction, allowing the paint to blot out in the desired portions to be blended. With the second paintbrush, stroke from the opposite edges inward, allowing the paint to blot out as it overlaps the previous color, creating a blended effect.

Painting on Silk

The banners in the photos on pages 21, 82, and 83 were created by painting on white silk satin. However, a purchased scarf blank may be used or experiment with different silk-blend fabrics.

Before the silk can be painted on, it must be stretched between stretcher bars, which may be purchased or made from lattice strips. Stretch the silk across the frame and secure with straight pins or staples. Make sure that the fabric paint selected is appropriate for silk.

To create a washed background, choose the desired colors and dilute each in a plastic cup. The amount of water used to dilute the paint will determine the softness of the color. It is best to use colors in an order that will blend well together. Use a foam brush for each different color. Have all colors and brushes ready to go as the paint cannot be allowed to set between colors. Start at the top of the fabric and brush across with desired color. Continue until the desired color is achieved. Immediately apply the next color, overlapping the first. Continue down to bottom of fabric.

The designs may now be transferred onto the silk. A charcoal pencil can be used to lightly draw the design onto the fabric or paint it free-hand. To achieve a soft look, paint the design when the silk is still wet from the background application. For a more determined line, wait until the silk is dry to paint the design. Use a full-pointed paintbrush to apply designs. Accents may be added with metallic or thicker paint.

To create a design that is more defined, such as the banner with the ribbon design on page 82, a resist must be used. A clear, water-soluble resist is best for this purpose. After the background wash has been applied and dried, transfer design with a charcoal pencil. Go around the design with the resist and let dry. This procedure allows painting within the lines without any bleeding. Paint individual designs as desired with any of the above methods.

The paint must now be set. One method is to use a hot iron placed directly on painted areas, slowly pressing and lifting from each area to the next. Another method is to place painted fabric in a clothsdryer on high for 45 minutes.

Painted fabrics may be cut and finished as desired.

Sponge Painting

Dip a small damp sponge brush into paint and blot onto paper, removing excess paint. Then, blot the surface of the object to be painted until desired coverage is achieved.

Stamping

This technique is used to create specific designs such as those on the Stamped Sunflowers banner on page 87.

1. Cut desired shape, such as a leaf shape, from dense craft foam.

2. Apply paint to foam using a paintbrush. If shaded stamping is desired, apply two or more colors to foam.

3. Stamp the surface of the object to be painted until desired design is achieved.

Embellishing with Dimensional Fabric Paint Pens
This technique is ideal for outlining, lettering, or creating raised accents on projects.

For paint pens, place tip of applicator onto project and squeeze gently to begin paint flow. Continue squeezing and moving paint pen along surface until desired look is achieved. Allow project to dry flat for 4 to 6 hours.

For fabric markers, follow manufacturer's instructions.

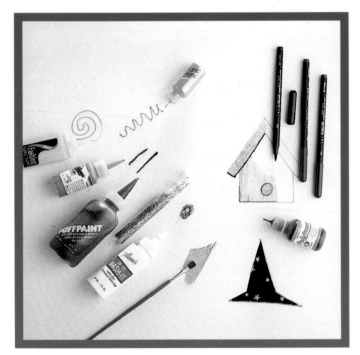

Woodcutting

1. Trace the pattern onto the wood using the patterns and chalk or transfer paper method on page 8.

2. Starting with an outside line near the edge of the wood to be cut, slowly ease the jigsaw into the wood. Continue cutting pattern, following traced lines.
Note: At a tight turn, back up about ½" and cut slightly outside the cut tracing line, creating a space to allow the blade to turn and complete the pattern.

3. Sand any rough edges

Displaying Banners

Suggestions for different ways to hang banners are given in the specific instructions for each project. Any project can adapt to most any way to hang it but the mounting is basically the same. Purchase an adjustable bracket for poles. An adjustable bracket will tilt 180-degrees so a banner can be mounted from a vertical or horizontal surface. Follow manufacturer's instructions for mounting bracket.

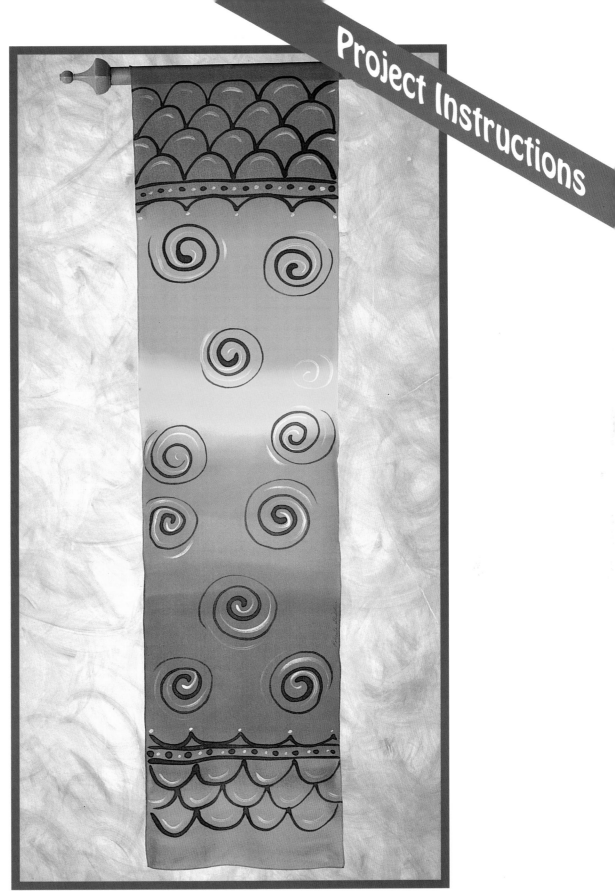

Painted Silk Banner instructions on pages 19 and 82.

Long Live the Queen

Materials For Banner
Rip-stop nylon fabrics: black (¼ yd.),
    blue (⅛ yd.), green (¼ yd.),
    hot pink (1⅜ yds.), red (⅛ yd.),
    white (¼ yd.), yellow (½ yd.)
Gold metallic fabric: 7" x 5"
Rip-away backing: 1¼ yds.
Flat back jewels: blue marquis (5), blue
    oval (2), clear heart (2), gold star (5),
    green oval (1), green rectangle (2), hot
    pink oval (2), hot pink round (2),
    red heart (1)
Gold-tone charm: 3" square
Ribbon, ⅛": blue (½ yd.), green (½ yd.),
    hot pink (¼ yd.)
Black thread

Materials For Hanger
Wooden dowel, ½" dia.: 34"
Wooden beads, 1" dia. with ½" dia. hole: 2
Gold cording: 1¼ yds.
Acrylic paint: if desired

Tools and General Supplies
Glue stick
Paintbrushes
Sewing machine
Straight pins
Tape
Tracing paper
Washable glue
Wipe-away marking pen

Instructions
All seams are ½" unless indicated otherwise.
Finished banner size is 27½" x 42½".

1. Enlarge pattern on page 90. Lay tracing paper over pattern and transfer all markings.

2. Cut a 31" x 46½" piece from hot pink fabric. This will be the banner. Center pattern vertically onto banner and mark placement as necessary. Remove pattern and cut out individual pieces.

3. Using the color pattern on page 90 as a guide, cut pieces from designated color of fabric. Use the glue stick to temporarily attach pieces to banner. If necessary, baste around larger sections to hold in place. Note: Textile medium mixed with black paint is an alternative to appliquéing lettering. Refer to general instructions if this method is preferred.

4. Place rip-away backing under entire banner and pin in place. Use a satin stitch and black thread to secure each piece to banner. When all pieces have been stitched in place, tear off backing.

5. Hem sides and bottom of banner ¾". Turn top edge down 2¼" and hem to form casing for dowel.

6. From blue ribbon, tie two small bows. Repeat with green ribbon. From hot pink ribbon, tie one small bow. Sew or glue the bows along ruffle of dress, referring to photo for placement.

7. With washable glue, attach jewels to queen as follows: Five blue marquis along crown, five gold stars above crown points, one hot pink round and one green rectangle for each earring, alternate ovals at bow centers, two clear hearts on shoes, and one red heart glued to gold-tone charm for brooch.

8. Paint dowel and wooden beads if desired. Insert dowel through top casing of banner. Wedge wooden beads onto each end. Tie gold cording to each end of dowel.

Wild and Crazy Mom!

For an additional Mother's day banner, try this Wild and Crazy Mom banner. The pattern is on page 120.

Best Witches

Materials For Banner

Cotton fabrics: black (1 yd.), black with gold
    stars (1 yd.), green (scrap),
    dk. green (scrap), lt. green (scrap),
    gold print ($\frac{1}{3}$ yd.), gold and purple
    stripe (scrap), purple ($\frac{1}{8}$ yd.), purple
    print ($\frac{1}{3}$ yd.), red (scrap)
Fusible interfacing: 1 yd.
Fusible webbing: $\frac{3}{4}$ yd.
Black thread
Florescent dimensional paint writers: black,
    gold, green, orange, red, yellow
Small amount of green raffia
Red glitter

Materials For Hanger

Broom with 40" handle

Tools and General Supplies

Iron and ironing board
Sewing machine
Scissors
Straight pins
Tacky glue
Tape
Tracing paper

Instructions

All seams are $\frac{1}{2}$" unless indicated otherwise.
Finished banner size is 33" x 36$\frac{1}{2}$".

1. Enlarge pattern on page 91. Lay tracing paper over pattern and transfer all markings.

2. Place pattern pieces, except cauldron front and back, and cape, onto fusible webbing and trace. Trim around patterns, cutting just the general shape, not the exact pattern. Using the color pattern on page 91 as a guide, iron fusible patterns onto the wrong side of designated color of fabric. Cut out the exact pattern from each material. Set aside.

3. Cut cauldron pattern from black and black with gold stars fabrics, and from fusible interfacing. Iron interfacing to the back of black fabric. Place the black with gold stars cauldron on top of interfacing, wrong side down. Pin in place. Surge around the cauldron through all thicknesses with a short stitch using the rollhem foot of sewing machine. Fold top edge under to back side 3$\frac{1}{2}$" and hem at that mark.

4. Lay the pattern pieces, except hat, nose, and shoes in place on the front of the cauldron, referring to photo and color pattern for placement. Pin in place. Iron on pattern pieces.

5. Cut a small handful of raffia 14" long. Tie in center with double thickness of thread. Stitch raffia to top of the head. Place hat on top of raffia and iron on. Iron nose in place over raffia. Note: Use a cloth when ironing over hat and nose to prevent raffia from burning.

6. Spread a thin layer of tacky glue over surface of red shoes. Sprinkle red glitter over glue. Press lightly with fingers to set glitter. Let dry completely. Shake off excess glitter. When dry, iron in place. Note: To prevent glitter from melting when ironing over shoes, cover with a cloth .

7. Sew a straight stitch around all pieces. Note: This stitch will be covered with paint in Step 9.

8. Sew a $\frac{1}{4}$" hem in smallest edge of cape. Gather this edge to measure 2" across. Stitch cape in place at witch's neck. Stitch cape down about 12" along back line of witch's dress.

9. Using florescent dimensional paint writers, outline all pieces with a coordinating or contrasting color of paint. Also, outline some of the print pattern on cape and hat. (Model has swirls outlined.)

Additional color idea for the Best Witches banner.

Oak Leaves & Acorns

Materials For Banner
Polished cotton fabrics: brown (¹/₈ yd.),
dk. brown (scrap), lt. brown (scrap),
green (¹/₄ yd.), dk. green (¹/₄ yd.),
tan (2 yds.)
Fusible webbing: 1 yd.
Matching thread for all fabrics

Materials For Hanger
Wooden dowel, 1" dia.: 36"
Wooden finials, 3" long with a ³/₈" peg
at base: 2
Wood stain
Acrylic sealer

Tools and General Supplies
Drill with ³/₈" bit
Iron and ironing board
Paintbrush
Pencil
Scissors
Sewing machine
Straight pins
Tracing paper
Wood glue

Instructions
All seams are ¹/₂" unless indicated otherwise.
Finished banner size is 20" x 23".

1. Enlarge pattern on page 100. Place tracing paper over enlarged pattern and transfer all markings. Cut out individual pieces.

2. Cut out two banner shapes from tan fabric. Set aside.

3. Place individual pattern pieces onto fusible webbing and trace. Trim around patterns, cutting just the general shape, not the exact pattern. Using the color pattern on page 100 as a guide, iron fusible patterns onto the wrong side of designated color of fabric. Cut out the exact pattern from each material.

4. Center and arrange all pieces onto right side of one tan piece, referring to pattern. Pin pieces in place. When all pieces are placed as desired, iron onto fabric, working a small section at a time.

5. Satin-stitch around all pieces with coordinating color of thread. Satin-stitch dark green leaves first, followed by light green leaves, dark brown acorns, light brown acorn caps, and brown stems.

6. Place both tan banner pieces right sides together. Stitch around curved edges. Turn right side out and press.

7. From tan fabric, cut five 5" x 7" pieces. On each piece, bring long edges together and sew a seam, forming straps. Turn and press. Fold each strap in half and pin in place along top of banner. Turning top edges of banner under ¹/₂", hand-stitch closed.

8. Drill a ³/₈" hole in both ends of dowel. Insert finials into ends of dowel. Stain and let dry. Apply acrylic sealer to dowel and let dry.

9. To hang banner, remove one finial and slip dowel through straps. Replace finial. Wood glue may be used to permanently hold finials in place.

Hurt not the earth, neither the animals, nor the trees.

Additional banner idea.
This Earth Day Banner pattern is on page 118.

Angel's Sing

Materials For Banner
Moire taffeta fabric: ivory (1/2 yd.)
Sheer fabric: ivory (1/2 yd.)
Sheer, shiny fabric: 5" square
Satin fabrics: pink (5" square), bright
    yellow (5" square)
Fleece batting: 1/2 yd.
Fusible webbing: 1/8 yd.
Lace, 2": ivory (1 1/3 yds.)
Thread: heavy gold, shiny ivory
Dimensional fabric pen: metallic gold

Materials For Hanger
Brass horn with rings for hanging: 26"
Decorative cording, 5/8" dia.: 36"
Matching tassels, 6": 2

Tools and General Supplies
Fray preventative
Iron and ironing board
Pencil
Scissors
Sewing machine
Sewing needle
Straight pins
Tape
Tracing paper
Transfer paper

Instructions
All seams are 1/2" unless indicated otherwise.
Finished banner size is 23" x 15".

1. Enlarge pattern on page 105. Transfer pattern and all markings to tracing paper. Cut out individual pieces from traced pattern.

2. Using scalloped banner pattern piece, cut one from fleece, two from taffeta, and two from sheer ivory fabric.

3. Apply fray preventative along the edges of sheer ivory pieces. Let dry.

4. Trace patterns for hair, face, and hands onto fusible webbing. Trim around patterns, cutting the general shape, not the exact pattern. Iron fusible hair pattern onto wrong side of bright yellow satin. Iron fusible hands and face patterns onto wrong side of pink satin. Cut out exact patterns from each fabric. Set aside.

5. Trace patterns for hair and face onto shiny, sheer fabric. Cut out and set aside.

6. To make background, place taffeta scallop pieces, right sides together, on top of fleece scallop piece. Pin through all three layers. Sew a 1/2" seam along scalloped edges and 6" in on each side of straight edge. Clip curves every 1/2" around scalloped edges. Turn and press. Blind-stitch top edge closed.

7. Transfer quilting lines onto background and machine quilt with shiny embroidery thread. With pins, mark placement of angel's head. Set aside.

8. Sew a medium zig zag stitch around all edges of sheer ivory scalloped piece, this now becomes the angel's dress. With scalloped edges pointing down, find the center of each piece and place on top of each other at base of head marking on quilted background. Bar tack across neckline about 1", letting fabric drape downward. Iron fusible hair and face patterns into place, overlapping neckline of dress. Note: Place a cloth between satin pieces and iron to prevent scorching of material.

9. Place the patterns from Step 5 over angel's head and pin in place. Satin-stitch around hair and face. With thick gold thread, stitch eyes and mouth onto face.

10. Fold corners of bottom layer of dress to the back and bring corners of top layer to the front. Pin in place. Referring to pattern for placement, iron pink satin hands in place. Satin-stitch around hands and sleeve markings.

11. Pin lace to back of quilted background along scalloped edge. Tack in place.

12. Place a yardstick across banner where lettering will go and mark with pins to produce a straight line. Lightly write the words "And The Angel's Sing" with pencil. If preferred, trace lettering from pattern and use transfer paper to transfer onto banner. Paint over letters with metallic gold fabric pen. Let dry.

13. With thick gold thread, sew five loops across the top of banner. Place cording through rings on horn and secure tassels to each end of cording. Slip horn through loops in banner.

29

Autumn Leaves Banner

Materials For Banner
Ultra suede (artificial) fabrics: cream ($^1/_6$ yd.), rust ($^1/_2$ yd.), lt. tan ($^1/_4$ yd.), tan ($^5/_8$ yd.), terra cotta (1$^1/_4$ yds.)
Assorted ribbons: 12 different textures, sizes, and colors ($^1/_2$ yd. each)
Sheer ribbon, 2": bronze ($^3/_4$ yd.)
Thread: to match ribbon colors, transparent
Glass pre-strung bugle beads, $^1/_4$": gold (1 yd.)
Glass pre-strung seed beads, 2mm: lt. green ($^1/_2$ yd.), rust (6 yds.)
Seed beads, 1mm: assorted fall colors
Fusible webbing: $^1/_2$ yd.
Acrylic paints: fall colors

Materials For Hanger
Wooden curtain rod with finials

Tools and General Supplies
Paintbrushes
Pencil
Scissors
Sewing machine
Sewing needle
Straight pins
Tracing paper

Instructions
All seams are $^1/_2$" unless indicated otherwise.
Finished banner size is 22" x 39".

1. Enlarge pattern on page 94. Place tracing paper over enlarged pattern and transfer all markings. Cut out traced patterns.

2. Trace leaves onto fusible webbing. Trim around leaves, cutting just the general shape, not the exact pattern. Using the color pattern on page 94 as a guide, iron fusible leaves onto the wrong side of designated color of ultra suede. Cut out the exact patterns from each material and set aside.

3. From terra cotta fabric, cut a 23$^1/_2$" x 40$^1/_2$" piece for back of banner, and a 5$^1/_2$" x 23$^1/_2$" strip for front of banner. From rust fabric, cut a 17" x 23$^1/_2$" piece. From tan fabric, cut a 20" x 23$^1/_2$" piece. From light tan fabric, cut five 3" x 6" pieces for hanging tabs.

4. Pin leaves randomly to tan piece. When desired placement is achieved, iron on. Straight-stitch around leaves with transparent thread. Stitch fall-colored seed beads in vine-like patterns on leaves.

5. Pin bronze sheer ribbon down center of terra cotta strip. Stitch down sides of ribbon with matching thread. Swirl 5 yards of rust seed beads down center of bronze ribbon. Pin in place. When desired pattern is achieved, sew beads using a grooved foot on sewing machine.

6. Pin $^1/_2$ yard lengths of ribbon and beads across rust section. When desired look is achieved, sew along edges of ribbons with matching thread. Sew beads in place as in Step 5.

7. Sew banner front together with tan fabric for top, terra cotta strip for center, and rust for bottom; see photo.

8. With right sides together, align long edges of each hanging tab. Stitch down long edge. Turn right side out and press. Fold tabs in half to form loops and pin across top of banner with loops pointing down. Pin banner backing on top of banner front with right sides together. Stitch around sides, leaving a 12" opening to turn. Turn right side out. Slip-stitch opening closed. Press if needed. Sew a straight stitch around banner $^1/_4$" in from edge. Hang banner from wooden curtain rod.

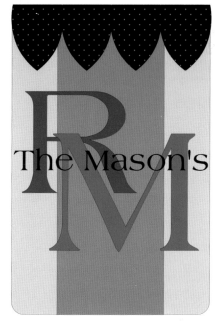

Additional banner idea.
This Family Banner pattern is on page 119. Personalize this banner using the accompanying alphabet also on page 119.

Winter Banners

Materials For Banners

Angel with Christmas Trees Banner
Cotton fabrics: black with gold stars
   (14" x 25"), plaid (8" x 11"), tan (5" x 12")
Muslin fabric: natural (scrap)
Pressed cotton batting: 22" x 14"
Buttons: assorted round natural (25),
   wooden heart (1), wooden stars (3)
Floss: black
Jute: 4-ply (5")
Twine: natural
Acrylic paints: beige, dk. green, metallic
   gold, dk. red
Fine-point permanent marker: black
Wooden wings: 11" x 4"
Large craft sticks: 6
Wire, 16 gauge: 7"

Stocking Banner
Cotton fabrics: red plaid (5/8 yd.),
   coordinating stripe (6" x 9"),
   coordinating checked (6" square)
Muslin fabric: natural (5/8 yd.)
Pressed cotton batting: 1/2 yd.
Buttons: wooden heart (3)
Floss: black
Jute: 4-ply (12")
Acrylic paints: dk. green, metallic gold

House Banner
Cotton print fabrics: black (scrap),
   black checked (3" square),
   blue (1/3 yd.), brown (scrap),
   gold (scrap), green (6" x 8"),
   red (6" x 8"), tan (3" square)
Pressed cotton batting: 8 1/2" x 11"
Floss: black
Fusible webbing: 8" x 10"

Mitten Banner
Cotton fabric: green plaid (³⁄₈ yd.)
Muslin fabric: natural (scrap)
Pressed cotton batting: 12" x 16"
Yarn: cream, green
Acrylic paint: dk. red
Index card
Tea bag

Reindeer Banner
Cotton fabrics: black (12" x 9"),
　　brown (6" x 4"), tan (scrap)
Pressed cotton batting: 12" square
Narrow leather trim: red (3")
Floss: black
Twine
Tiny bead: cream
Tiny buttons: black (2)
Jingle bells, ¹⁄₄": 3
Dried cranberries: 30
Large craft stick

Spool Snowman
Jute: 4-ply (1 yd.)
Acrylic paints: black, cream, orange, red
Acrylic spray: matte finish
Wooden spools, 2": 3

Materials For Hanger
Wooden dowel, ¹⁄₂" dia.: 48"
Large metal star
Buttons, ⁵⁄₈" dia.: 8
Twine: natural (1 spool)
Jute: 4-ply (2 yds.)
Acrylic paint: dk. red

Tools and General Supplies
Craft knife
Drill: ¹⁄₈" and ¹⁄₄" bits
Glue: tacky, wood
Needles: darning, sewing
Paintbrushes: flat, stencil
Pencil
Pliers
Scissors
Straight pins
Tracing paper
Transfer paper

Instructions
Banners may be made and hung individually or collectively. All seams are ¹⁄₂" unless indicated otherwise.
<u>Angel with hanging Christmas trees</u>
Finished banner size is 13" x 13".

1. From black with gold star fabric, cut two 12¹⁄₂" x 13¹⁄₂" pieces. Cut one 12¹⁄₂" x 13¹⁄₂" piece from batting. Place batting between the wrong sides of both black with gold star pieces. Pin together. With twine and darning needle, sew long, uneven basting stitches ¹⁄₄" in from edge. This will be the banner background.

2. Place wooden wings onto tan fabric and trace. Cut out fabric wings and glue onto wooden wings with tacky glue. Using a ¹⁄₈" drill bit, drill holes in wings at different intervals, making about five holes in each wing.

3. For angel's dress, cut a triangle shape from plaid fabric that is 1¹⁄₂" wide at the top, 6" wide at the bottom, and 9" high. Using this as a pattern, cut another triangle from batting.

4. From muslin fabric, cut two 2¹⁄₂"-diameter circles. Place circles right sides together and stitch around edges. Pull fabrics apart in the center and clip a small slit through one layer. Turn right side out and lightly stuff with batting. Whip-stitch opening closed. On other side, draw a face with black marker; see pattern on page 95.

5. Paint heart button dark red and star buttons beige.

6. Cut craft sticks into pieces to make three trees, each consisting of one trunk and five branches. Assemble trees by laying the trunk vertically and wood-gluing the branches across trunk. Wrap intersections with twine and tie off ends. Paint both sides of trees dark green and let dry. Carefully drill a ¹⁄₈" hole in top of each tree to thread twine for hangers. Glue buttons randomly on both sides of trees.

7. With metallic gold paint, dry-brush the edges of wings, heart, stars, and trees.

8. Lay wings in place on background piece. Sew to banner with twine through drill holes.

9. Place plaid dress piece over batting and pin together. With twine, sew heart in center and stars across bottom. Pin dress in place on top of wings. With black floss, stitch around dress through all layers with long, uneven stitches until reaching the wings;

stitch only through dress in the wing area. Glue head in place.

10. Cut five 1" lengths of jute. Glue in place forming hair.

11. With pliers, twist wire into a circle. Stitch at halo position with twine.

12. Thread lengths of twine through tree holes and hang from bottom of banner.

Stocking Banner
Finished banner size is 8" x 20".

1. Enlarge stocking pattern on page 95. Place tracing paper over enlarged pattern and transfer all markings. Cut out patterns.

2. From red plaid fabric, cut two stocking patterns. From striped fabric, cut one cuff. From checked fabric, cut one toe and heel. From muslin, cut two stocking patterns. From batting, cut two stockings, one cuff, one toe, and one heel.

3. Paint heart buttons dark green and highlight with metallic gold.

4. For front of stocking, layer as follows: one muslin stocking (right side down), one batting stocking, and one red plaid stocking (right side up). Place cuff, toe, and heel batting in position and layer appropriate fabrics on top. Using two strands of black floss, stitch bottom edge of cuff and inside edges of toe and heel in place with cross- and straight stitches. Stitch wooden heart buttons across cuff. Layer stocking front onto other piece of muslin, batting, and plaid. Starting at the top of the stocking, blanket-stitch through all layers around edges, leaving top open. At top edge of stocking, blanket-stitch around front and back separately.

5. Fold jute in half and stitch to top of stocking for hanger.

House Banner
Finished banner size is 8½" x 11".

1. Enlarge pattern on page 95. Place tracing paper over enlarged pattern and transfer all markings. Cut out patterns.

2. Turn patterns over and trace onto fusible webbing. Trim around patterns, cutting just the general shape, not the exact pattern. Using color pattern on page 95 as a guide, press fusible patterns onto appropriate color fabric. Cut out exact patterns.

3. Cut two pieces of blue fabric and one piece of patting, each 8½" x 11". Arrange design onto one of the blue pieces and iron in place. Using two strands of black floss, sew a running stitch around each piece. Sew two long stitches across window forming window panes.

4. Pin batting between wrong sides of both blue fabrics. Use four strands of floss to stitch through all layers around outside edges.

Mitten Banner
Finished banner size is 11" x 7".

1. Steep tea bag in boiling water until tea looks fairly strong. Dip muslin scrap into tea and let set for several minutes. Remove fabric. Rinse and wring to remove excess tea. Set aside and let dry, allowing fabric to stay wrinkled.

2. Enlarge pattern on page 95. Place tracing paper over pattern and trace each piece. Cut out patterns.

3. From green plaid fabric, cut four mittens. From batting, cut two mittens. Cut one heart from dry tea-dyed muslin and one heart from batting.

4. For front of mitten layer one plaid mitten, batting, and another plaid mitten. Using cream yarn, stitch long vertical stitches across top edge. Stitches do not have to be all the same length, but should be about ¼" apart. Repeat with green yarn between cream stitches.

5. Transfer "joy" stencil pattern onto index card. Cut out stencil with craft knife. Place stencil over muslin heart. Stencil pattern with dark red paint. Remove stencil and let dry.

6. Place stenciled heart onto heart batting and position on mitten. Stitch around heart through all layers with four strands of black floss, using cross- and straight stitches.

7. For back of mitten layer plaid mitten, batting, and last plaid mitten. With cream yarn, slip-stitch across top edge. Place front and back mittens together and slip-stitch around edges, leaving top open.

Reindeer Banner
Finished banner size is 5" x 7".

1. Cut black fabric into two pieces, each 5⅜" x 8". From batting, cut one piece the same size.

2. Enlarge reindeer pattern on page 95. Place tracing paper over enlarged pattern and trace each piece.

34

Cut out patterns. From brown fabric, cut reindeer body. From tan fabric, cut hooves and antlers. From batting, cut one of each pattern.

3. Layer and finish reindeer banner in same manner as angel with trees banner, using black floss stitches around reindeer and twine blanket stitches around edges.

4. Sew leather trim around reindeer's neck forming harness. Stitch bells in place around harness. Sew tiny buttons in place for eyes and tiny bead for nose.

5. String dried cranberries onto an 8" length of twine. Secure ends to top of banner on each side.

6. Cut a craft stick to fit across the top back of banner. Glue in place to stabilize banner.

Spool Snowman

1. For body, paint two spools cream. For head, paint one spool with top half black and bottom half cream. Paint a red strip around black portion of head forming hat. On cream portion of head, paint black dots for eyes and mouth, paint nose orange like a carrot. On body, paint black dots for buttons down both spools. When dry, spray with matte acrylic.

2. Tie a knot in one end of jute. Thread bottom body

onto jute. Tie another knot and thread on middle body. Tie another knot and thread on head. Make a loop and tie last knot.

Instructions for Hanger

1. Thin down dark red paint with a small amount of water and brush onto dowel. Let dry.

2. Place dowel on work surface and position banners as desired; see diagram. Mark placement where the holes need to be drilled. Drill marked holes with $1/8$" drill bit. With a $1/4$" drill bit, drill a hole 1" in from each end, these holes will have jute threaded through them to hold entire hanger.

3. To attach each piece to hanger, thread a needle with two strands of twine, about 1 yard each. Place a button on top of first drill hole. Take needle and twine down through one hole of button, through the hole in dowel, through the piece to be hung, back up through the hole in dowel, and out through second hole in button. Slide off needle and pull ends until even. When all banners and buttons have been threaded onto dowel, adjust them to be even across the top edge. Tie a knot on top of each button to secure. Tie a bow and trim off excess.

4. Thread jute through larger holes on ends of dowels. Knot each end.

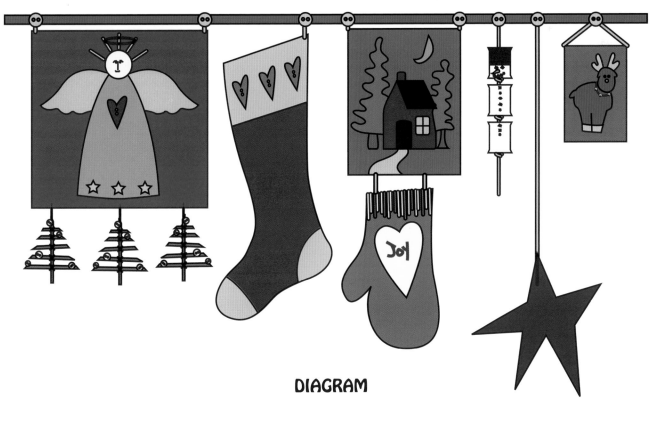

DIAGRAM

The following are additional ideas to make these beautiful lace banners:

- Change the flowers and colors to match those of any wedding. Also, attach momentos such as napkins or invitations from the wedding.

- For a Victorian Christmas banner, stitch flowers in Christmas colors and add holly, ivy, and berries as additional adornments.

- Salute mother on Mother's day by stitching her favorite flowers. Personalize the banner by replacing the wording with "We Love Mother" and "Love," "Joy," and "Caring."

Wedding Banner

Materials For Banner

Metallic fabric: gold (1/2 yd.)
Moiré faille fabric: ecru (1/2 yd.)
Old lace: scraps
Venice lace, 3/4" wide: ivory (2 1/2 yds.)
Fusible interfacing: 1 yd.
Quilt batting: 6" square
Posterboard: 6" square
Thin organdy ribbons: 9mm pale olive (6 yds.),
    8mm, iris cross-dyed (4 1/2 yds.),
    5mm, olive green (4 1/2 yds.)
Wide organdy ribbons: 2", iris cross-
    dyed (3 yds.), 1", olive green (3 yds.),
    5/8", pale olive (3 yds.)

Materials For Embroidery

Embroidery floss: metallic gold strand (5 yds.),
    DMC 327 (2 yds.), DMC 781 (2 1/2 yds.),
    DMC 895 (1 1/2 yds.), DMC 3051 (2 1/2 yds.)
Silk ribbon, 4mm: gold (27"), hand-dyed,
    lavender-shaded (1 1/2 yds.), pale
    olive (1 yd.), purple (1/2 yd.), violet (1 1/2 yds.)
Silk ribbon, 7mm: dk. green (1 yd.), olive
    green (3 yds.)
Wired ribbon, 5/8": dk. green (1 yd.),
    lt. green (25")
Hand-dyed, bias-cut ribbon: purple (65")
Rayon ribbon, 3/8": olive green (15")
Velvet ribbon, 3/16": hunter green (10")
Satin ribbon, 1/8": dk. green (15")
Cotton ribbon, 9mm: olive green (30")
Decorative ribbon, 1 1/2": red (1 1/8 yds.),
    white (1 yd.)
Flat braid: gray (1 yd.), lavender (1/2 yd.),
    olive green (1/2 yd.)
Beads: assorted sizes and colors

Tools and General Supplies

Embroidery transfer pen
Embroidery hoop
Embroidery needles
Pencil
Scissors
Sewing machine
Tracing paper
Transfer paper

Instructions

All seams are 1/2" unless indicated otherwise.
Finished banner size is 35" x 19" for all three.

1. Enlarge large and small crest patterns on page 40. Place tracing paper over enlarged patterns and transfer all markings.

2. From metallic gold fabric and interfacing, cut two small crests and one large crest adding 1/2" to all edges of crests. Cut ecru moiré faille for crest backs, adding 1/2" to all edges; set aside. Fuse interfacing crests to wrong side of gold metallic crests. Using tracing paper pattern, trace exact stitch lines on gold fabric. Collage lace scraps onto crest fronts as desired. Machine-stitch in place with narrow zig zag stitches. Press. Machine zig zag outer edges of each crest front.

3. Using a transfer pen, transfer each embroidery design onto each crest front. Embroider designs according to patterns on pages 40-43.

4. With right sides together, pin each crest front to each back. Stitch together along exact stitching line, leaving a 3" opening in one side seam. Trim seams to 1/8". Clip corners and curves. Turn. Slip-stitch opening closed. Press flat avoiding embroidery and ribbon work.

5. Pin Venice lace onto side edges of each crest, overlapping front of crests 1/4". Machine-stitch lace to fronts with a narrow zig zag stitch. Press.

6. Cut narrow sheer ribbons into three 24" lengths. Handling lengths as one, tie a bow at center of length. Tack bow to top edge of one small crest at center front. Drape tails to back of crest and secure in place. Repeat to make a bow on second small crest.

7. Cut narrow sheer ribbons into three 28" lengths. Loop ribbons together, leaving one end of each free. Stitch ribbons together at top of loops, forming tassel. Tack looped ribbons to back of one small crest at bottom point. Cut a scrap of ribbon 5" long. Stitch to center top edge on back side of crest for hanger. Repeat to make a tassel and hanger on second small crest.

8. To make hanger on large crest, tie a loop at center of 1/4"-wide ivory cording. Extend and stitch cording tails to back side of large crest at top center.

9. Handling the three wide sheer ribbons as one, tie together forming a six-looped bow with 28" tails. Glue bow to ivory cording at top knot. Drape ribbon tails down each side of crest, knotting ribbons together and tacking to top side edges. Knot ends of each ribbon length separately.

10. Cut three plaques from posterboard, following pattern on page 40. Cut three plaques from ecru moiré, adding 1" to all edges. Center and transfer lettering to each piece of moiré. Embroider lettering.

11. Pad each plaque with batting trimmed flush to edge. Center and wrap embroidered lettering to padded cardboard. Flute pale olive, gold-edged ribbon to each plaque, gluing to back side. Glue Venice lace to top and bottom edges of plaques on back sides. Cup each plaque and glue in place; see photo on page 36.

12. Hang banners together; see photo on page 36.

EMBROIDERY STITCHES

Bullion Lazy Daisy
Complete as a lazy daisy, but tack with a bullion stitch.

1. Bring needle down and up through fabric, but do not pull through.
2. Loosely wrap ribbon around needle tip twice. Holding finger over wrapped ribbon, pull needles through ribbon. Insert needle again, pulling to fabric back.
3. Completed bullion stitch.

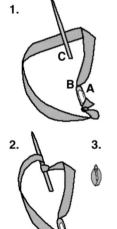

Colonial Knot
1. Come up at A. Drape ribbon in a backward "C". Place the needle through the "C".
2. Wrap the ribbon over the needle and under the tip of the needle forming a figure 8. Holding the knot firmly on needle, insert the needle through the fabric close to A. Hold the ribbon securely until the knot is formed on top of the fabric.

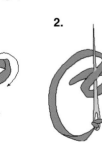

Couching
1. Complete a straight stitch base by coming up a A and going down at B at a desired length. Keep the ribbon flat and loose.
2. Make a short, tight straight stitch across the ribbon base to couch the straight stitch. Come up a C on one side of the ribbon. Go down at D on the opposite side of the ribbon. The tight, short stitch across the ribbon will cause the ribbon to gather and pucker. The straight stitch base is tacked at varying intervals.

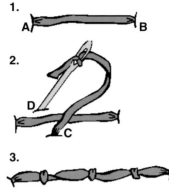

3. Completed couching stitch.

Fluting
Attach one ribbon end to fabric, loop to desired length and glue. Repeat making a series of even loops.

Gathered Leaf
Cut a 5" length of ribbon for each leaf. Fold ribbon in half, matching raw ends. Beginning at fold, gather-stitch along one salvage edge. Pull gathers for medium fullness. Secure thread. Open leaf. Gather-stitch along raw edges. Pull thread tight; secure. Hide raw end under petals when stitching to fabric.

Lazy Daisy
1. Bring the needle up at A. Keep the ribbon flat, untwisted, and full. Put the needle down through fabric at B and up through at C, keeping the ribbon under the needle to form a loop. Pull the ribbon through, leaving the loop loose and full. To hold the loop in place, go down on other side of ribbon near C, forming a straight stitch over loop.
2. Completed Lazy Daisy Stitch.

One-Twist Ribbon Stitch

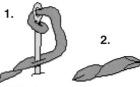

1. Follow instructions for the ribbon stitch, adding a twist in the ribbon before pushing the needle back down.
2. Completed One-Twist Ribbon Stitch

Pointed Petal/Leaf

Cut a 2½" length of ribbon. Fold ribbon at a 45-degree angle, then fold again to form a triangle. Stitch across ends and gather tightly. Wrap bottom of leaf several times with thread. Secure thread. Tuck raw ends of leaf under, then stitch in place.

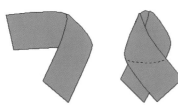

Ribbon Stitch

1. Come up through fabric at the starting point of stitch. Lay the ribbon flat on the fabric. At the end of the stitch, pierce the ribbon with the needle. Slowly pull the length of the ribbon through to the back, allowing the ends of the ribbon to curl. If the ribbon is pulled too tight, the effect of the stitch can be lost. Vary the petals and leaves by adjusting the length, the tension of the ribbon before piercing, the position of piercing, and how loosely or tightly the ribbon is pulled down through itself.

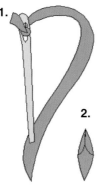

2. Completed ribbon stitch.

Rose (White)

1. For white rose, cut a 7" length of white ribbon. Press in half, matching long edges. Turn one end down. Stitch. Gather-stitch remaining length, tapering at end. Pull gathers as tight as possible and stitch ruffle around center post. Stitch onto fabric. Glue stamens to center.

2. Cut four 4" lengths of ribbon. Stitch a squared-off petal as in diagram. Pull gathers to measure

1¾". Secure thread. Hide raw edges of ribbon while stitching each petal around center ruffle to fabric.

Rose (Red)

1. For the red rose, repeat Step 1 of white rose using red ribbon.
2. Cut three 3" lengths of ribbon and fold as in diagram. Gather-stitch raw edges. Pull thread tight and secure. Hide raw edges of ribbon while stitching petals under center ruffle to fabric.

Rose Bud

Fold a 5" length of red or white ribbon as in the pointed petal/leaf. Tuck raw edge under as appliquéing to fabric.

Ruched Ribbon

Cut one each of 20" and 24" lengths of ribbon. Starting ½" from one end, lightly mark ⅜" intervals with dull pencil along one edge. On remaining edge, lightly mark ⅜" intervals, but offset the marks so that they occur halfway between the marks on the opposite edge. Using one strand of floss in matching color, sew a running stitch in a zig zag pattern connecting all the pencil marks. Pull floss tails to gently gather into cupped ruffles.

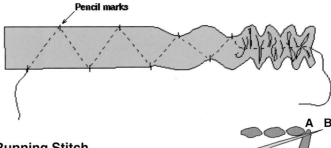

Running Stitch

A line of straight stitches with an unstitched area between each stitch. Come up at A and go down at B.

Stem Stitch

Working from left to right, make slightly slanting stitches along the line of the stem. Come up at A and insert needle through fabric at B. Bring needle up at C, halfway between A and B. Make all stitches the same length. Insert needle through fabric at D, half the length of the stitch beyond B. Bring the needle up at the middle of previous stitch and continue in the same manner.

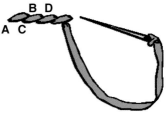

Stitched Pointed Petal/Leaf

1. Thread ribbon onto large darning needle. Bring ribbon to surface at A. Miter ribbon at B. Stitch back into fabric next to A. Tack point of petal with floss.
2. Completed Pointer Petal/Leaf.

Violet

Press bias ribbon in half, matching raw edges. Cut into seven 6½" lengths. Fold each length in half, matching short ends. Stitch together along short ends. Gather-stitch along raw edges. Pull thread tight and secure. Repeat for remaining six lengths. Stitch each violet in place through center. Stitch a colonial knot in center of each violet using gold 4mm ribbon.

devotion

faithful

unity

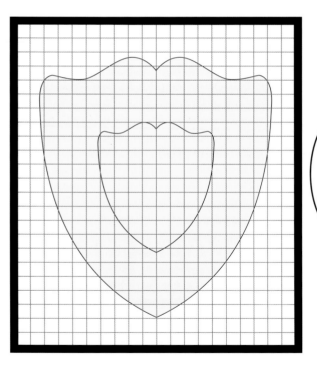

BANNER CREST PATTERN

PLAQUE PATTERNS

EMBROIDERY GUIDE

Using three strands of DMC 327, stitch running stitches to outline letters on plaque piece. Weave gold stranded floss through running stitches.

From This Day

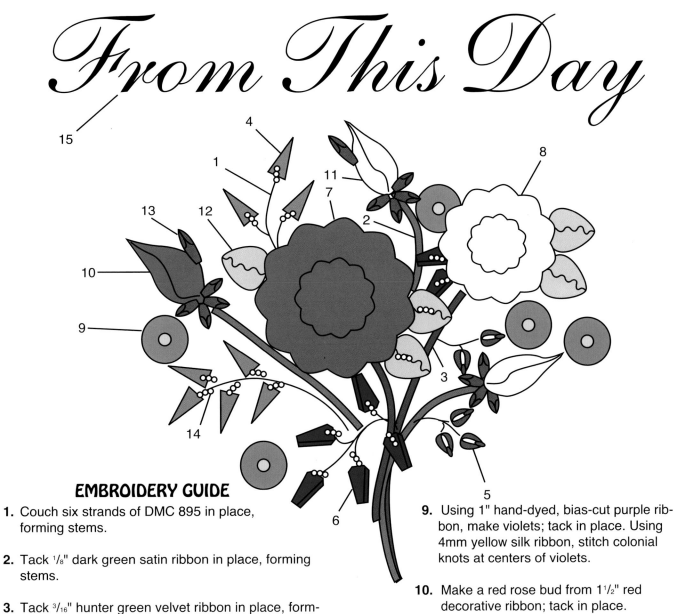

EMBROIDERY GUIDE

1. Couch six strands of DMC 895 in place, forming stems.

2. Tack ⅛" dark green satin ribbon in place, forming stems.

3. Tack ³/₁₆" hunter green velvet ribbon in place, forming stems.

4. Using 9mm olive green cotton ribbon, make stitched pointed petals/leaves.

5. Using 7mm olive green silk ribbon, stitch lazy daisy stitches.

6. Using ⅝" dark green wired ribbon, make pointed petals/leaves; tack in place.

7. Make a red rose from 1½" red decorative ribbon; tack in place.

8. Make a white rose from 1½" white decorative ribbon; tack in place.

9. Using 1" hand-dyed, bias-cut purple ribbon, make violets; tack in place. Using 4mm yellow silk ribbon, stitch colonial knots at centers of violets.

10. Make a red rose bud from 1½" red decorative ribbon; tack in place.

11. Make a white rose bud from 1½" white decorative ribbon; tack in place.

12. Using ⅝" light green wired ribbon, make gathered leaves; tack in place.

13. Using 7mm olive green silk ribbon, stitch one twist ribbon stitches.

14. Stitch assorted beads in place.

15. Using six strands of DMC 781, stitch running stitches to outline letters. Weave 4mm purple silk ribbon through running stitches, then weave gold stranded floss through running stitches, criss-crossing previous weave.

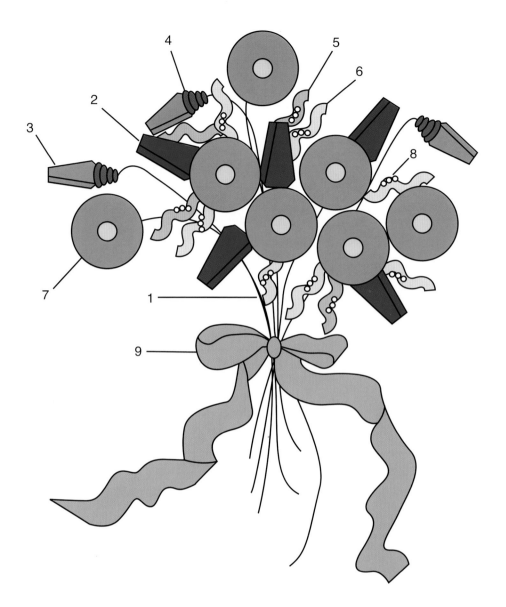

EMBROIDERY GUIDE

1. Couch six strands of DMC 3051 in place, forming stems.

2. Using ⁵⁄₈" dark green wired ribbon, make pointed petals/leaves; tack in place.

3. Using 1" hand-dyed, bias-cut purple ribbon, make pointed petals/leaves; tack in place.

4. Using 7mm olive green silk ribbon, stitch ribbon stitches to form bud calyx.

5. Using lavender flat braid, ruche ribbon; tack in place.

6. Using gray flat braid, ruche ribbon; tack in place.

7. Using 1" hand-dyed, bias-cut purple ribbon, make violets; tack in place. Using 4mm gold silk ribbon, stitch colonial knots at centers of violets.

8. Tack assorted beads in place.

9. Make a bow from 15" of ³⁄₈" olive green rayon ribbon; tack in place.

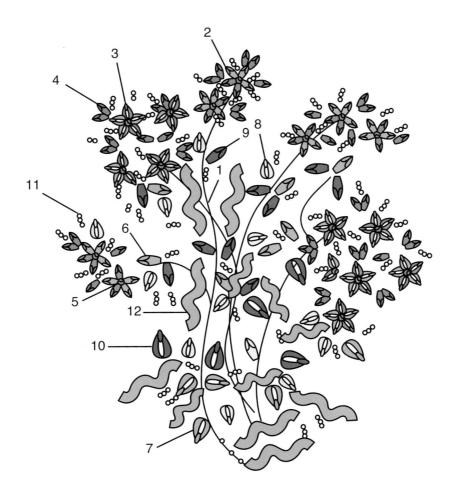

EMBROIDERY GUIDE

1. Stem-stitch three strands of DMC 3051, forming stems.

2. Using 4mm hand-dyed, lavender-shaded silk ribbon, stitch ribbon stitches.

3. Using 4mm hand-dyed, lavender-shaded silk ribbon, stitch lazy daisy stitches.

4. Using 4mm purple silk ribbon, stitch ribbon stitches.

5. Using three strands of DMC 327, stitch colonial knots at centers of flowers.

6. Using 7mm olive green silk ribbon, stitch ribbon stitches.

7. Using 7mm olive green silk ribbon, stitch bullion lazy daisy stitches.

8. Using 4mm pale olive silk ribbon, stitch bullion lazy daisy stitches.

9. Using 7mm dark green silk ribbon, stitch ribbon stitches.

10. Using 7mm dark green silk ribbon, stitch bullion lazy daisy stitches.

11. Tack assorted beads in place.

12. Using olive green flat braid, ruche ribbon; tack in place.

Welcome Home Birdhouses

Materials For Banner
Heavyweight canvas fabric: $^2/_3$ yd.
Thread to match fabric
Acrylic paints: black, blue, gold, dk. gray,
     green, maroon
Permanent marker: black
Grommets: 3

Materials For Hanger
Wooden birdhouses: $5^1/_2$" tall (2); $3^1/_2$" tall (1)
Wooden slat: $^3/_8$" x 1" x $18^1/_2$"
Acrylic paints: same colors as above
Acrylic sealer
Black tie wire: 3 yds.

Tools and General Supplies
Drill with $^1/_{16}$" bit
Grommet tool
Paintbrushes
Pencil
Pliers
Scissors
Sewing machine
Stencil brushes
Tracing paper
Transfer paper
Wire cutters

Instructions
All seams are $^1/_2$" unless indicated otherwise.
Finished banner size is $18^1/_2$" x 32".

1. Enlarge pattern on page 89. Place tracing paper over enlarged pattern and transfer all markings.

2. From heavyweight canvas, cut a piece 34" x 22". Working with the canvas vertically, bring top corners together and crease, forming a point. Cut away corners at crease mark. Hem all edges of banner under 1".

3. Center traced pattern onto canvas banner. Slip transfer paper between banner and pattern. With pencil, trace over pattern lines.

4. Using a stencil brush and the dry brush technique, paint birdhouses following color pattern on page 89. Shade birdhouses so that the edges appear darker. Let dry.

5. Outline all lines with permanent black marker.

6. Insert grommets in top of banner, one on each side and one in center.

7. Paint wooden birdhouses and slat as desired and let dry. Apply acrylic sealer.

8. Drill a hole in the roof and bottom of each birdhouse. Drill a hole in the center and on each side of wooden slat.

9. With wire cutters, cut a 24" length from tie wire. Thread wire through hole in center of slat, down through smaller birdhouse roof, out through bottom, and through center grommet in banner. Adjust birdhouse by bending wire with pliers and curling ends.

10. Using the remaining wire, mark center. Thread wire through left grommet on banner, up through one larger birdhouse bottom, through the roof, through left hole in slat, down through right hole in slat, down through remaining birdhouse roof, out through bottom, and through right grommet on banner. Bend wire with pliers to hold birdhouses and slat in place and curl ends.

Additional banner idea.
This Welcome Little One banner pattern is on page 114.

Noah's Ark

Materials For Banner

Cotton print fabrics: black (4" x 9"),
    black-checked (2" x 9"), black-
    striped (4" x 7"), blue (4" x 18"), dk.
    blue (6" x 18"), brown ($1/2$ yd.),
    brown (4" square), burgundy ($1/3$ yd.),
    gold (7" x 12"), gold (4" square),
    gray (9" square), green ($3/8$ yd.),
    green (4" square), peach (4" square),
    pink (scrap), red ($1/2$ yd.),
    tan (6" square), tan-checked ($2 1/4$ yds.),
    tan-striped (4" x 6"), white (6" square),
    yellow ($1/2$ yd.)
Extra-wide bias tape: 4 yds.
Jute: $1/2$ yd.
Thread to match all fabrics
Heavy string: 4 yds.
Bird button
Wooden anchor: 3"
Small amounts of wooly hair: brown, gray
Fusible webbing: 3 yds.
Rip-away backing: 2 yds.
Acrylic paints: black, brown, pink, white
Textile medium
Hula hoop: 32" dia.

Tools and General Supplies

Dressmaker's pen
Iron and ironing board
Paintbrushes
Pencil
Safety pin
Scissors
Sewing machine
Straight pins
Tracing paper

Instructions

All seams are $1/2$" unless indicated otherwise.
Finished banner size is 31" x 31".

1. Enlarge pattern on page 92. Place tracing paper over enlarged patterns and transfer all markings. Cut out traced patterns.

2. Trace patterns onto fusible webbing. Trim around patterns, cutting just the general shape, not the exact pattern. Using the color pattern on page 92 as a guide, iron fusible patterns onto the wrong side of designated color of fabric. Cut out the exact patterns from each material.

3. Use $2 1/4$ yards of tan-checked fabric for backing and base. Fold in half with right sides together and cut edge aligned with cut edge. Center hula hoop on fabric. Trace around hoop with dressmaker's pen. Adding 4" to all edges, trace another circle. Cut two circles from largest pattern.

4. For the base, lay one of the circles on work surface, right side up. Pin pattern pieces in place referring to pattern. When placed as desired, iron to base.

5. Pin rip-away backing to the back of base. Satin-stitch around all pieces with matching thread. Remove rip-away backing.

6. Transfer face markings. Mix paints with textile medium and paint following colors in pattern. Paint wooden anchor black and highlight with white.

7. Hand-stitch wooly hair and beard in place. Thread 12" of jute through hole in anchor and tie a knot in one end. Stitch opposite end to edge of ark. For nest, fold remaining jute in half and hand-stitch so it curves in elephant's trunk. Sew bird button into nest.

8. Place base circle and backing circle with wrong sides together. Use extra-wide bias tape to bind circles together. Leave opening where ends meet. Attach large safety pin to one end of heavy string and thread through opening. Pull string slightly to gather fabric. Insert hula hoop and pull string tightly. Knot off string.

Additional color idea for the Noah's Ark banner.

47

come often
to my garden,

for your pleasure
is my
greatest joy of all.

Garden Banner

Materials For Banner

Banner fabric: tan (1/2 yd.)
Organdy ribbon, 1 1/2": peach (1 yd.)
Artificial fruit and vegetables
Miniature frogs: 2
Miniature garden tools: 2
Straw hat: 5"
Wooden spool: 2 1/2"
Acrylic paints: dk. brown, dk. green-yellow
Acrylic spray: clear
Wood sealer
Wooden frame: 18" square with 1 1/2" molding

Materials For Hanger

Brass chain: 12"
Eye screws, 1 13/16": brass (2)

Tools and General Supplies

Awl
Blow dryer
Industrial-strength adhesive
Iron and ironing board
Masking tape
Paintbrushes
Pencil
Pliers
Saw
Staple gun and staples
Tracing paper
Transfer paper

Instructions

All seams are 1/2" unless indicated otherwise.
Finished banner size is 18" x 18".

1. Make a mixture from dark brown and dark green-yellow paint and thin down with water. Wash frame, tools, fruits and vegetables, and hat with mixture. Let dry.

2. Cut banner fabric to 18" square. Fold edges in 1/2" with right sides together and stitch all the way around. Iron fabric.

3. Spray tools, fruits and vegetables, and hat with acrylic clear spray. Coat frame with wood sealer.

4. Enlarge and transfer lettering pattern on page 106 to front of banner fabric. With slightly diluted dark green-yellow paint, paint the lettering.

5. Tape banner to back of frame, making sure that lettering is straight. Staple in place, pulling tightly. Spray banner with water and dry with blow dryer to create a tight fit.

6. Saw spool in half lengthwise. Tie ribbon around straw hat.

7. With industrial-strength adhesive, attach hat, tools, fruits and vegetables, spool, and frogs to frame referring to photo for placement. Let set-up completely.

8. With awl, make two holes in top of frame. Insert eye screws. Using pliers to open chain links, insert one end of chain into each eye screw. Separate chain in center and adjust lengths as desired.

9. Hang from outdoor light pole or as desired.

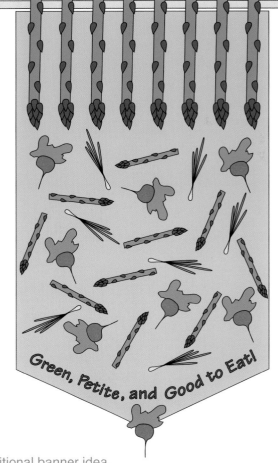

Additional banner idea.
This Good To Eat banner pattern is on page 121.

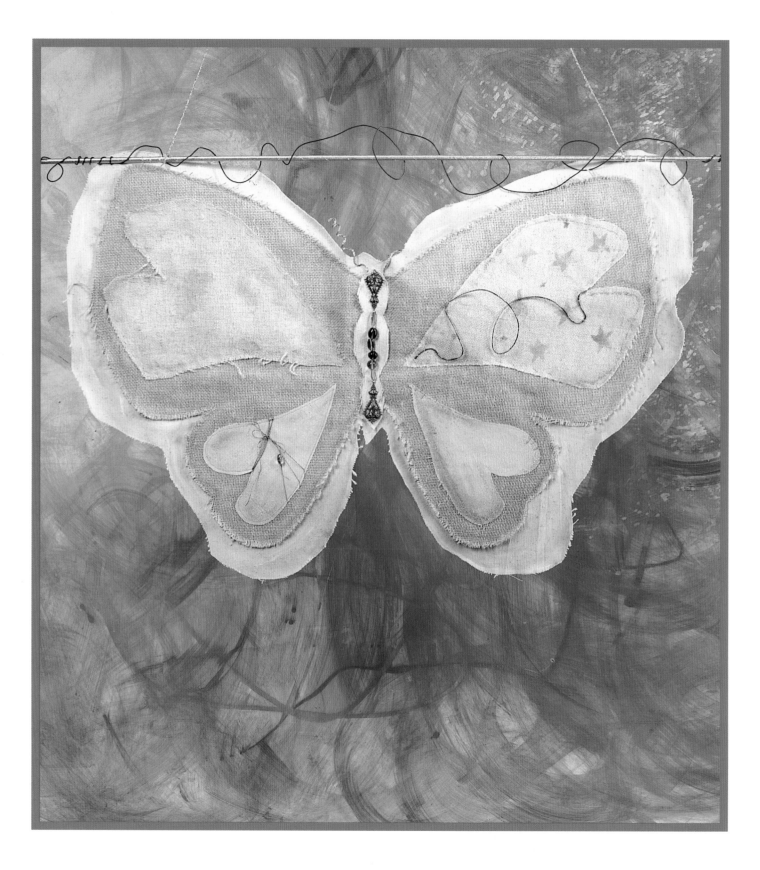

Butterfly Banner

Materials For Banner
Burlap fabric: natural (¹/₄ yd.), tan (⁵/₈ yd.)
Canvas fabric: natural (³/₄ yd.)
Muslin fabric: natural (9" x 16")
Wired trim: gold (12")
Thread: metallic gold, metallic gold with
    black, tan
Assorted glass beads: golden colors (7)
Victorian charms: gold (2)
Acrylic paints: cream, metallic copper,
    metallic gold
Glitter paint: gold
Fusible interfacing: heavy (1¹/₄ yds.)

Materials For Hanger
Ribbon, 1¹/₂": metallic gold (2 yds.)
Wired trim: gold (¹/₂ yd.)
Wooden dowel, ¹/₄" dia.: 36"
Bailing wire, 16 gauge: 2¹/₂ yds.

Tools and General Supplies
Iron and ironing board
Paintbrush: stiff
Pencil
Pliers
Scissors
Sewing machine
Sewing needle
Straight pins
Tacky glue
Tracing paper

Instructions
All seams are ¹/₂" unless indicated otherwise.
Finished banner size is 31" x 21".

1. Enlarge pattern on page 105. Place tracing paper over enlarged pattern and trace each piece. Cut out individual patterns.

2. From tan burlap, cut one large butterfly. From natural burlap, cut two large hearts and one butterfly body. From muslin, cut two small hearts. From fusible interfacing, cut two large hearts, two small hearts, and one large butterfly. Press interfacing to back of designated pieces.

3. Lay canvas on work surface and place burlap butterfly in center. Draw an uneven butterfly shape that is about 1"- 2" larger than burlap butterfly. Cut out canvas butterfly.

4. Wrap one small heart loosely with metallic gold with black thread. Slip on a bead. Tie a bow. Pin heart to lower left side of burlap butterfly. Stitch around heart ¹/₄" in from edge with tan thread. Pin other hearts in place. Hand-stitch hearts to burlap butterfly with gold metallic thread. Use a variety of stitches for a different look. Stitch butterfly body to center of burlap butterfly.

5. Pin burlap butterfly in center of canvas butterfly. Sew around burlap ¹/₄" in from edge with tan thread.

6. Glue Victorian charms to top and bottom of butterfly's body. Thread beads to fit in between charms and stitch in place. Curl wired gold trim to resemble antennae and stitch in place.

7. On left large heart, antique by painting edges with cream paint. On right large heart, randomly paint gold and copper stars. On small right heart, highlight with gold and copper paint. Highlight all hearts with gold glitter paint.

8. To cover dowel with gold ribbon, cut one edge of ribbon at an angle. Glue to end of dowel, using angled end as a straight edge. Wrap ribbon evenly and tightly around dowel and glue opposite end. Trim off excess.

9. Twist bailing wire around dowel with pliers, tighter on the ends and loosely in the center. Tie wired gold trim to each end of dowel for hanger. Stitch dowel to butterfly with metallic gold thread.

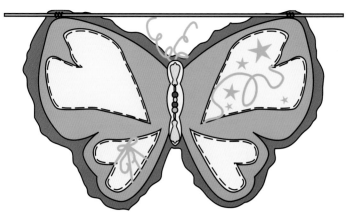

Additional color idea for the Butterfly Banner.

Sun Banner

Materials For Banner
Cotton fabric: dk. gold (1½ yds.)
Muslin fabric: ½ yd.
Thread: dk. gold, transparent
Acrylic paints: black, blue, lt. blue, brown,
    dk. brown, gold, orange, pink, lt. pink,
    purple, rust, tan, white, yellow
Gesso
Spray glitter
Textile medium
Permanent marker: black

Materials For Hanger
Any flag pole

Tools and General Supplies
Paintbrushes
Pencil
Ruler
Scissors
Sewing machine
Straight pins
Tracing paper
Transfer paper

Instructions
All seams are ½" unless indicated otherwise.
Finished banner size is 34" x 23".

1. Enlarge sun patterns on page 93. Place tracing paper over enlarged patterns and transfer all markings. Set aside.

2. Stretch muslin over a protected surface. With pencil, draw boxes onto muslin in the following sizes: 6" x 11", 7½" x 5¾", 8¼" x 7¼", 16" x 7", 6½" x 14½", and 6" x 10½". Paint inside all boxes with a mixture of gesso and textile medium. Let dry.

3. To transfer patterns into appropriate boxes, insert transfer paper between muslin and pattern and trace all markings.

4. Paint each design, referring to photo and color pattern. Several techniques may be used to create a different style for each sun. Try finger-painting, dry-brushing, shading, outlining, glitter highlights, bold colors, or soft washes.

5. Cut out each box. For banner front, cut a 45" x 54" piece from banner fabric. Place banner front on work surface right side up. Arrange and pin boxes onto banner, referring to photo for placement. When desired spacing is achieved, sew designs to banner using a straight stitch and transparent thread.

6. Cut banner shape, leaving a 1½" border on top, bottom, and right sides, and a 4½" border on left side. Using this as a pattern, cut another shape from banner fabric. Place both pieces right sides together and stitch around three sides, leaving left side open. Turn banner right side out.

7. Hem open edge under ½". Hem under again 1½" to form a casing for flag pole. Whip-stitch top of casing closed to avoid banner slipping down pole.

Additional banner idea.
This A Day At The Beach banner pattern is on page 116.

Fishing Banner

Materials For Banner

Cotton fabrics: purple print (³/₄ yd.), gold
  print (³/₄ yd.), gray print (³/₄ yd.), gray
  and purple variegated (³/₄ yd.)
Muslin fabric: ³/₄ yd.
Fusible webbing: ³/₄ yd.
Thread: gray, purple
Button, 1" : variegated gray
Button, ¹/₂" : black

Materials For Hanger

Old fishing pole
Fishing line

Tools and General Supplies

Iron and ironing board
Scissors
Sewing machine
Sewing needle
Straight pins
Tape
Tracing paper

Instructions

All seams are ¹/₂" unless indicated otherwise.
Finished banner size is 27" x 26".

1. Enlarge pattern on page 98. Lay tracing paper over pattern and transfer all markings. Cut out traced pattern pieces.

2. Trace patterns onto fusible webbing. Trim around patterns, cutting just the general shape, not the exact pattern. Using the color pattern on page 98 as a guide, iron fusible patterns onto the wrong side of designated color of fabric.

3. Cut out the exact patterns from each material. Place pieces onto 24"-square of muslin, referring to photo and color pattern for placement. Pin in place.

4. Iron pattern pieces onto muslin.

5. Satin-stitch around all pieces, except purple, with gray thread. Satin-stitch around purple pieces with purple thread.

6. Cut one 4" x 24" strip each from purple print fabric and gold print fabric. From gray and purple variegated fabric, cut two 4" x 24" strips.

7. Pin gold strip down one side of banner with right sides together. Sew a seam down this edge. Fold border in half and press. Fold raw edge under ¹/₄" and whip-stitch to back. Repeat for other side with purple strip. Repeat for top and bottom with variegated strip.

8. Sew small button on top of larger button and stitch in place for eye.

9. Attach banner to old fishing pole by stitching loops in banner with fishing line and hanging through rings on pole.

Additional banner idea.
This Hats Off To Dad banner pattern is on page 120.

RV Banner

Materials For Banner

Cotton print fabrics: black (6" square),
blue (1/8 yd.), blue check-print (1/8 yd.),
blue star-print (1 3/4 yds.), brown (scrap),
gray (2 scraps), green (5/8 yd.),
red (1/2 yd.), yellow (3 yds.)
Button, 1/2": black
Thread: navy (3 large spools), red,
transparent
Fusible interfacing: 1 5/8 yds.
Fusible webbing: 2 yds.
Rip-away backing: 1 1/2 yds.
Suspender clips: 5

Tools and General Supplies

Iron and ironing board
Pencil
Sewing machine
Sewing needle
Scissors
Straight pins
Tracing paper
Transfer paper

Instructions

All seams are 1/2" unless indicated otherwise.
Finished banner size is 57" x 28".

1. Enlarge pattern on page 99. Place tracing paper on top of enlarged pattern and transfer all markings. Cut out traced patterns.

2. Turn patterns over and trace onto fusible webbing. Trim around the patterns, cutting just the general shape, not the exact pattern. Using the color pattern on page 99 as a guide, iron the fusible patterns onto the wrong side of designated color of fabric. Cut out exact patterns.

3. For background, cut a 55" x 25" piece from blue star-print fabric. From yellow fabric, cut one 55" x 25" piece, two 56" x 9" strips, and two 30" x 9" strips.

4. Arrange fabric patterns onto background piece. Iron in place.

5. Pin rip-away backing onto back of background piece. Satin-stitch around all patterns with navy blue thread. Option: Hand-stitch around patterns with a blanket stitch and navy floss.

6. Trace and transfer lettering for family name, city, and state. Machine-embroider lettering with red thread. Option: Hand-embroider lettering using red floss.

7. Remove rip-away backing.

8. Iron fusible interfacing to the wrong side of the 55" x 25" piece of yellow fabric. Pin yellow back piece to front of banner with wrong sides together. With transparent thread, sew a 1/2" seam around all sides.

9. Fold all yellow strips in half lengthwise with wrong sides together and press. Pin one 56" strip to the back top edge of banner with all raw edges together. Sew a 5/8" seam. Repeat for bottom strip. Fold border piece open and press. Fold pieces over to front side so that border measures 2" wide and press. Pin in place. Top-stitch very close to inside edge of borders. Trim ends so that they are even with sides. Repeat for side borders with 30" strips. Hand-sew open ends closed.

10. From yellow fabric, cut five pieces 1 1/2" x 2". Fold each piece in half lengthwise with wrong sides together. Sew a 1/4" seam around long side and one short side. Turn right side out. Hem opening and press. Slip a tab through each suspender clip. Fold in half and sew clips evenly across top of banner. Use clips to attach banner to any canvas awning.

Additional color idea for the RV Banner.

Biker Banner

Materials For Banner
Canvas fabric: black (¹/₂ yd.)
Thread: black
Fabric paints: navy blue, gold, green, maroon, white
Grommets: black (5)

Materials For Hanger
Wooden curtain rod with finials: 30"
Chain link: black (1 yd.)
Screw hooks: black (5)
Acrylic paint: black
Wood sealer

Tools and General Supplies
Awl
Grommet tool
Paintbrushes
Pencil
Pliers
Scissors
Sewing machine
Tracing paper
Transfer paper: white

Instructions
Finished banner size is 33" x 16".

1. Enlarge pattern on page 97. Place tracing paper over enlarged pattern and transfer all markings.

2. Cut black canvas to measure 34" x 18". Center traced pattern onto front of canvas. Insert transfer paper between canvas and pattern and trace design.

3. Paint design onto canvas following pattern. Let dry.

4. Hem banner 1" around all sides.

5. Starting 1" from left top edge, attach grommets every 8".

6. Lay rod across top of banner and mark placement of grommets. With awl, make holes at marks and insert screw hooks.

7. Paint rod with black paint. When dry, coat with wood sealer.

8. With pliers, separate chain links into five equal pieces. Insert a chain into each grommet. Hang chains from hooks on rod.

Keep On Trikin'

Keep on Trikin'

Materials For Banner
Cotton fabric: white (¹/₂ yd.)
Fusible interfacing: ¹/₂ yd.
Embroidery floss: blue, green, red,
    yellow, (4 yds each)
White thread
Acrylic paints: blue, green, orange, purple,
    red, yellow

Materials For Hanger
Bicycle flag pole

Tools and General Supplies
Iron and ironing board
Masking tape: ⁵/₈"
Paintbrush: #4 flat
Pencil
Sewing machine
Sewing needle
Stencil brush
Tracing paper
Transfer paper

Instructions
All seams are ³/₈" unless indicated otherwise.
Finished banner size is 20" x 12".

1. Enlarge pattern on page 97. Cut out two flag shapes from white fabric. Zig zag-stitch around raw edges to prevent fraying.

2. Tape pattern onto paper-covered work surface. Tape one white flag over pattern. Stencil lines should show through fabric. Begin placing masking tape along lines extending past edges of fabric. Tape every other line in one direction, then other direction.

3. Starting at point of flag, stencil diamonds with yellow first, fading gradually to red, then to purple, blue, and green. Add yellow to last row of green. Repeat for other white flag. Let dry 24 hours. Remove tape and set paint with hot iron, using pressing cloth over painted flag. Transfer letter pattern to painted side of flags. Paint letters orange. Let dry.

4. Cut out one flag from fusible interfacing. Iron onto wrong side of one painted flag. Place flags right sides together and sew with ³/₈" seam, leaving a 2" opening to turn. Clip corners; turn, and press. Slip-stitch opening closed. Topstitch around flag ¹/₄" in from edges.

5. Place six strands of each color embroidery floss together and knot one end. Tie another knot 9" from end. With needle and thread, stitch second knot securely to lower corner of flag. Twist and tack floss at 1" intervals around long sides of flag. Knot end of floss at top corner and secure. Measure 9" and knot again. Cut off. Cut two 9"-lengths of floss and knot each end. Tack one at each corner to use for ties. Attach to flag pole on child's tricycle.

Additional banner idea.
This Queen of the Road banner pattern is on page 121.

Northwoods Cabin Banner

Materials For Banner

Canvas fabric: off-white (1/2 yd.)
Denim fabric: lt. blue (1 1/2 yds.)
Fleece blanket fabric: southwestern-
    print (1 yd.)
Thread: lt. blue, tan
Thin twine: natural (1 spool)
Old buttons: shades of tan (40-45)
Star buttons, 1 1/2": 2
Wooden shank button: 1"
Small amount of doll hair: white
Handmade (textured) paper:
    black (3 1/2" x 5")
Pine tree picks: 2
Acrylic paints: black, gold, dk. peach, rust
Redwood deck sealer
Redwood stain
Balsa wood: 1/4" x 4" x 6"
Twigs, 15" long: approx. 50
Wooden cutouts: coyote (5"), moon (4")
Tooling copper: 3 1/2" x 5"

Materials For Hanger

Chain link: 12" length
Eye screws, 1 3/4": 4
Small finishing nails
Wood: 5/8" x 13" x 40"

Tools and General Supplies

Awl
Craft knife
Fray preventative
Glue: decoupage, wood
Hammer
Needle, large-eyed
Paintbrushes
Pencil
Pliers
Sandpaper
Scissors
Scroll saw
Sewing machine
Tracing paper
Transfer paper
Wire cutters

Instructions

**All seams are 1/2" unless indicated otherwise.
Finished banner size is 24 1/2" x 35".**

1. Enlarge pattern on page 101 and make template. Referring to pattern for hole placement, use awl to make eight holes in moon and four holes in coyote. Note: Moon and stars may be cut from balsa wood if pre-made pieces cannot be found.

2. Paint moon gold. Paint stars dark peach. Paint coyote dark peach and highlight with rust and black. Let dry. If banner will be hung outdoors, coat pieces with deck sealer.

3. Trace house shape onto canvas and cut out. Apply fray preventative to edges of canvas and let dry.

4. From denim, cut a piece 21" x 23 3/4". From fleece, cut two strips 21" x 6" for top and bottom border, two strips 24 3/4" x 3" for sides, and four pieces 3" x 6" for corners. When cutting the fleece, incorporate the pattern so that the pieces contrast appropriately. Sew a corner piece to each end of top and bottom strips. Set fabrics aside.

5. Place canvas house on work surface. Place twigs onto canvas following pattern and trimming to size with wire cutters. Remove twigs from canvas. Place canvas house on front of denim and sew in place with zig zag stitches.

6. Sew fleece border strips around edges of denim, sides first then top and bottom.

7. Place twigs on work surface in the shape of the house. One at a time, stitch them to the canvas with twine, using a long cross-stitch. For the roof outline, whip-stitch twigs in place.

8. Cut three twigs; one 5 3/4" long, one 7" long, and one 11" long. Cut pine picks apart and twist them around twigs, forming trees. Whip-stitch trees in place on sides of log house.

9. Sew moon into place with twine, cross-stitching through holes. Sew coyote in place with a buttonhole stitch through holes. Sew stars in place. With pencil, draw a path from doorway to bottom corner. Sew buttons in place, overlapping as necessary.

10. From balsa wood, cut a 4" x 1" strip. Paint name on sign in black. With awl, make two holes on each side. Sew onto house with twine through holes.

11. Cut a small piece of balsa wood for chimney. With awl, make two holes on each side. Paint brown and let dry. Sew onto house with twine through holes. Sew white hair to top of chimney to resemble smoke.

12. For doorway, decoupage black handmade paper to tooling copper. Let dry. With awl, punch holes around top and sides 1/2" apart. Punch two holes in doorknob area. Cut twigs to fit sides and top of doorway. With twine, sew door and twigs onto log house using a whip-stitch. Sew wooden shank button in place for doorknob.

13. From denim, cut a piece for back 1/2" bigger all around than front. Cut five 10" x 3" pieces for tabs.

14. On each tab, fold long edges in 1/2" and press. Fold in half again. Sew around tabs 1/4" in from edges with tan thread. Fold tabs in half, forming loops. Pin along top front of banner with right sides together and loops pointing down. Top-stitch along edge.

15. Place banner front and back with right sides together. Stitch around sides and top. Carefully turn right side out and hand-stitch bottom edge closed. Machine-stitch around inside of border.

16. Transfer moose shape to wood. Cut out moose shape with scroll saw. From remaining wood, cut two pieces 4" x 26". Sand all edges of wood. Paint wood with redwood stain.

17. Center letter pattern onto one wood piece. Insert transfer paper between wood and pattern and trace letters. Paint letters black. When dry, coat all wood with redwood deck sealer.

18. Nail and wood-glue moose to top center of "WELCOME" board. On bottom of board, measure in 5" from each end and make a small hole with awl. Repeat on top of other board. Slip banner onto board. Insert eye screws into holes. Separate chain in half and attach to eye screws to hang.

Clubhouse Banner

Materials For Banner
Large T-shirt
Nylon fabric: green: 20" x 15"
Cotton fabric, white: 8" x 12"
Fusible webbing: $^1/_2$ yd.

Materials For Hanger
Tree branch
Rope: 3 yds.

Tools and General Supplies
Cardboard: large enough to fit inside shirt
Dimensional fabric pen: shiny black
Iron and ironing board
Pencil
Scissors
Transfer paper

Instructions
Finished design size is 10" x 11".

1. Enlarge pattern on page 102. Place tracing paper over enlarged pattern and transfer all markings. Cut out traced pattern.

2. Place pattern pieces onto fusible webbing and trace. Trim around patterns, cutting just the general shape, not the exact pattern. Iron frog pattern onto wrong side of green fabric. Iron cloud and eyes onto wrong side of white fabric. Cut out exact patterns from fabrics.

4. Arrange fabric patterns onto front of T-shirt. Iron in place.

5. Place a large piece of cardboard inside of T-shirt to provide a flat surface for painting. Outline cloud and write lettering with shiny black dimensional fabric pen. Work from top to bottom and left to right to prevent smearing. Outline frog eyes, filling in pupils. Continue following pattern lines to complete frog. Let dry 24 hours.

6. Hang T-shirt from tree branch with rope.

Harvest Angel Banner

Materials For Banner
Cotton fabric: tan checkered-print, (1 yd.)
Thread: tan
Acrylic paints: navy blue, brown, dk. brown,
    forest green, ivory, mauve, lt. peach,
    rust, tan, lt. tan, yellow, dk. yellow
Textile medium
Fine-point permanent marker: black

Materials For Hanger
Wooden dowel, $^1/_2$" dia.: 44"
Decorative metal vine: 36"
Twine

Tools and General Supplies
Darning needle
Iron and ironing board
Paintbrushes
Pencil
Scissors
Sewing machine
Tracing paper
Transfer paper

Instructions
All seams are $^1/_2$" unless indicated otherwise.
Finished banner size is 34" x 32".

1. For banner, cut tan checkered fabric to measure 36" square. With tan thread, sew around three sides 1" in from raw edges. Fray fabric around the three sides by pulling threads.

2. Enlarge pattern for harvest angel on page 96. Transfer enlarged pattern onto banner with transfer paper. Iron banner and stretch tight over protected surface with unfrayed edge as top of banner.

3. To begin painting, all paint must be mixed with textile medium, following manufacturer's instructions. Paint design following color pattern on page 96. When paint is dry, outline details with black marker.

4. Hem top of banner under $^1/_2$". Hem under again 1$^3/_4$", forming a casing for dowel. Insert dowel through casing. With twine, sew metal vine in place across top of banner.

Flannel Shirt

Materials For Banner
Flannel shirt
Leather-look vinyl fabric: black (12" x 18")
Thread: black
Fusible webbing: 12" x 18"

Materials For Hanger
Brackets with hardware: black (2)
Sturdy sawtooth hangers: 2
Toy rifle
Wood stain
Wooden dowel: to fit inside toy rifle barrel
Wood: $^5/_8$" x $3^1/_2$" x 40"

Tools and General Supplies
Hammer
Iron and ironing board
Paintbrush
Pencil
Screwdriver
Sewing machine
Straight pins
Tracing paper

Instructions
Finished design size is 13" x 13".

1. Enlarge pattern on page 102. Place tracing paper over enlarged pattern and transfer all markings. Cut out traced patterns.

2. Trace patterns onto fusible webbing. Trim around patterns, cutting just the general shape, not the exact pattern. Iron fusible patterns onto the flannel side of black vinyl. Cut out exact patterns from vinyl.

3. Pin vinyl patterns to back of flannel shirt. Turn shirt inside out and apply iron to area where patterns are placed. Turn shirt right side out. Satin-stitch around patterns.

4. Apply wood stain to board.

5. Glue dowel inside toy rifle. Slip rifle through sleeves of flannel shirt. Place rifle across board and mark measurements for bracket placement. Attach brackets to board. Attach sawtooth hangers to back of board. Hang rifle from brackets.

Everybody Needs Their Spot

Materials For Banner
Cotton fabrics: 2 different green prints (10"
    square each), solid red (15" square),
    red and black print ($1/2$ yd.), red print
    (13" square)
Tiny buttons: black (4)
Floss: black
Thread: black
Acrylic paints: black, blue, brown,
    dk. brown, red, tan
Textile medium
Permanent marker: black
Fusible webbing: $1/2$ yd.
Grommets: 2
Bird with cherries pin or ornament

Materials For Hanger
Acrylic paint: olive green
Acrylic sealer
Wood primer: white
Wood: $3/4$" x 7" x 15"
Wooden knob: 2" dia.
Wooden post: $1^1/2$" x $1^1/2$" x 46"
Small eye hooks: silver (2)
Small link chain: silver (12")
Head screws, $2^1/2$": 2

Tools and General Supplies
Drill with $1/4$" bit
Grommet tool
Industrial-strength glue
Iron and ironing board
Needle
Paintbrushes
Pencil
Pliers
Sandpaper: med. grit
Saw
Scissors
Screwdriver
Sewing machine
Straight pins
Tracing paper
Transfer paper

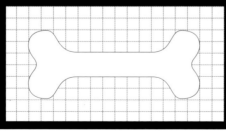

BONE PATTERN

Instructions

All seams are ¹⁄₂" unless indicated otherwise.
Finished banner size is 14¹⁄₂" x 16".

1. Enlarge pattern on page 106. Place tracing paper over enlarged pattern and trace individual pieces. Cut out patterns.

2. For banner background, cut two large crest patterns from red and black print. Place pieces right sides together and sew around edges, leaving a 4" opening at top. Turn right side out and whip-stitch opening closed. Press.

3. Turn remaining patterns over and trace onto fusible webbing. Trim around design, cutting just the general shape, not the exact pattern.

4. Referring to color pattern on page 106, iron fusible patterns onto the wrong side of designated color of fabric. Cut out exact lines. Note: Where cat's tail comes off the banner about 1¹⁄₂", a piece of matching fabric should be fused onto the back so that the banner will have a finished look from the back side.

5. Pin motifs onto banner background referring to pattern for placement. Iron in place.

6. Paint ears, nose, spots, and collar onto dog with acrylic paints mixed with textile medium. Paint nose and ears onto cat. When dry, outline with black marker.

7. Trace and transfer letters onto banner. Outline letters with black marker.

8. Satin-stitch around motifs with black thread. Stitch whiskers with black floss. Sew tiny black buttons in place for eyes. Attach bird to banner. Make two grommet holes in the top of banner.

9. For hanger, enlarge bone pattern on opposite page. Transfer design onto pine and cut out shape. Cut one end of post into a point. Sand pieces as necessary.

10. Paint all wood with primer. Let dry. Wash all wood with diluted olive green paint. Let dry. Coat wood with acrylic sealer.

11. Drill one hole 4" from top of post, centering and drilling all the way through. Drill another hole 3" below first hole. Insert screws through holes. Screw on bone horizontally. Glue wooden knob onto top of post and let dry.

12. Screw eye hooks to bottom of bone, spacing 6¹⁄₂" apart. With pliers, separate chain into two equal pieces. Attach chains to eye hooks and through grommet holes in banner.

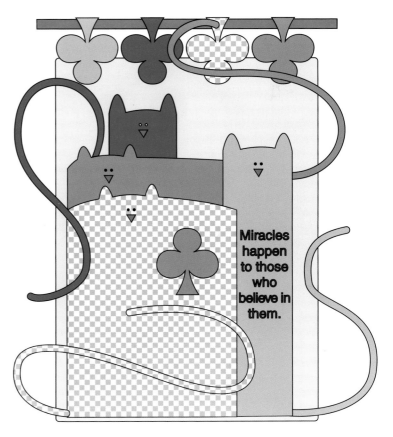

Additional banner idea.
This St. Patrick's Day Cats banner pattern is on page 114.

Birds of a Feather

Materials For Banner

Heavyweight canvas fabric: 1/2 yd.
Cotton fabrics: black (5" x 6"), checkered-
    print (1" x 16"), coordinating print for
    border (1/8 yd.), gold (5" x 6"),
    rust (5" x 6"), various prints (3 scraps)
Cording, 1/4" dia.: (32")
Embroidery floss: black
Thread to match all fabrics
Fusible webbing: 18" x 5"
Permanent marker: black

Materials For Hanger

Wooden dowel, 1/4" dia.: 28"

Tools and General Supplies

Iron and ironing board
Pencil
Sewing machine
Sewing needle
Scissors
Straight pins
Tracing paper
Transfer paper

Instructions

All seams are 1/2" unless indicated otherwise.
Finished banner size is 11" x 14".

1. Enlarge pattern on page 106. Place tracing paper over pattern and transfer all markings. Cut out traced patterns.

2. Trace patterns onto fusible webbing. Trim around patterns, cutting just the general shape, not the exact pattern. Using the color pattern on page 106 as a guide, iron fusible patterns onto the wrong side of designated color of fabric.

3. Cut out the exact patterns from each material. From heavyweight canvas, cut a piece 11" x 14". Pin pattern pieces lengthwise onto canvas, referring to photo and color pattern for placement.

4. Place checkered-print strip on work surface with right side up. Place cording in center of strip (16" of cording will be hanging out). Fold fabric over cording

and sew down side of cording with zipper foot. Sew across cording where fabric ends. Peel fabric down onto uncovered cording. Cut off excess cording. Cut covered cording into appropriate lengths for each perch. Pin in place, wedging one end under bird bodies. Tack bottom ends of perch to canvas.

5. Iron pattern pieces in place.

6. Satin-stitch around all patterns with matching thread. Satin-stitch a small eye in each bird.

7. From border fabric, cut two 2" x 14" strips, and two 2" x 11" strips. On each strip, fold long edges to center and press. Fold in half again and press. Pin both side strips and bottom strip to sides of banner. Sew in place, mitering corners. Place top strip in place and sew, leaving ends open to insert wooden dowel.

8. Position transfer paper between banner and traced letters. With pencil, transfer letters to banner. Trace over lettering with permanent black marker. With black embroidery floss, hand-sew a straight stitch around lettering.

Additional banner idea.
This Spring Duck banner pattern is on page 113.

Teatime Cat Banner

Materials For Banner

Cotton fabrics: blue (²/₃ yd.), blue with
    star-print (²/₃ yd.), brown-print (4" square),
    gold-print (6" square), green-
    print (3" square), orange-print (3" square),
    purple-print (3" square), red-
    print (3" square), rust (13" square)
Embroidery floss: black, green, lt. orange,
    yellow
Thread: blue
Yarn: lt. orange
Sunflower buttons: 5
Buttons, ⁵/₈": brown (2)
Fusible webbing: ¹/₃ yd.
Acrylic paint: ivory
Plastic stencil sheet

Materials For Hanger

Wood: 1" x 1" x 36"

Tools and General Supplies

Craft knife
Darning needle
Iron and ironing board
Pencil
Sewing machine
Scissors
Stencil brush
Tracing paper

Instructions

All seams are ¹/₂" unless indicated otherwise.
Finished banner size is 24" x 23".

1. Enlarge pattern on page 104, and make template. From plain blue and blue with stars fabrics, cut a 24" square. From blue with star-print fabric, cut ten hanger patterns from template.

2. Trace bird, cat, and cup patterns from template onto fusible webbing. Trim around patterns, cutting just the general shape, not the exact pattern. Using the color pattern on page 104 as a guide, iron fusible patterns onto the wrong side of designated color of fabric. Cut out the exact patterns from each material.

3. Trace picket fence pattern onto plastic stencil sheet. Cut out stencil with craft knife. Spray back of stencil with temporary adhesive. Using 24" blue with star piece for banner front, position picket fence. Stencil with ivory paint. Let dry.

4. Arrange fusible patterns in place on banner, referring to pattern. Iron on.

5. Hand-stitch around cat, bird, and cups with two strands black floss. Stitch stems with twelve strands of green floss. Stitch flowers with twelve strands of yellow floss. Cut 12 strands of light orange floss 2" long. Lay across cat's face in whisker position. With black floss, secure whiskers in center and continue stitching to form a mouth. Stitch french knots for eyes. Sew brown buttons to centers of yellow flowers.

6. Transfer lettering from template onto front of banner. With light orange yarn, stitch lettering.

7. Place two hanger strips right sides together. Sew around edges with a ¹/₄" seam, leaving straight short edge open. Repeat for remaining eight hanger strips. Turn pieces right side out and press. Top-stitch around hangers ¹/₄" in from edges.

8. Place banner front and plain blue backing with right sides together. Insert hangers between both fabrics across top edge. The straight edge of hanger should be even with the top edge, leaving the pointed end hanging down in between fabrics. Sew a ¹/₂"seam around edges, leaving a 6" opening on one side. Turn right side out and press. Whip-stitch opening closed.

9. Fold hangers over onto front and secure in place with sunflower buttons.

10. Insert 36" wood piece through hangers and hang as desired.

73

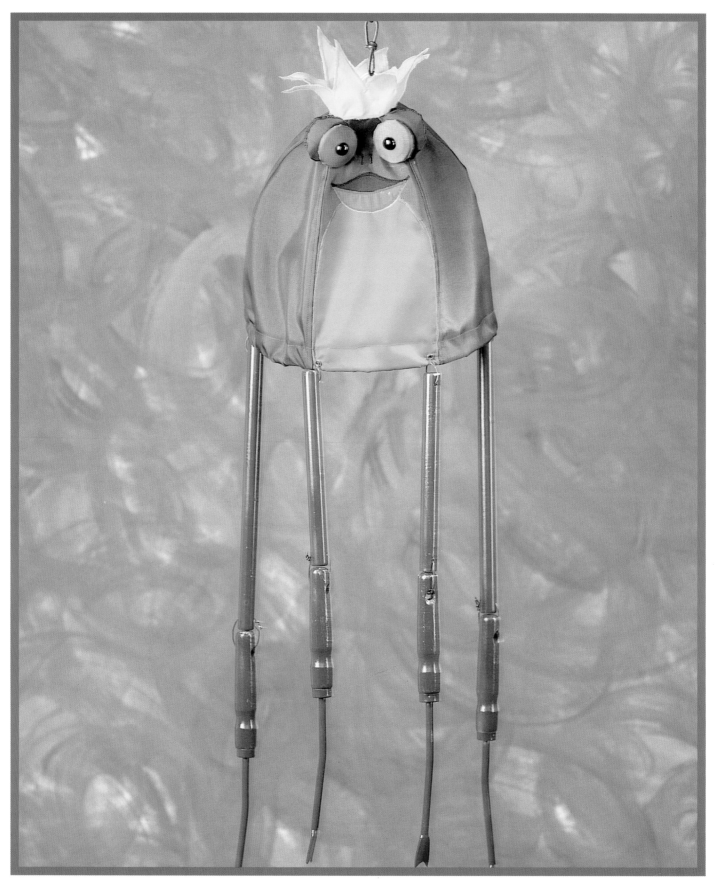

Frog Banner

Materials For Banner

Rip-stop nylon fabrics: black (scrap),
   dk. green ($\frac{1}{2}$ yd.), lime green (6" x 10"),
   hot pink (scrap), purple (8" x 4"),
   yellow (18" x 8")
Batting: small amount
Buttons, $1\frac{3}{4}$" with rounded surface: (2)
Small shank: black (2)
Heavy thread
Thread to match all fabrics
Spray enamel with rust preventative:
   dk. green
Aluminum pipe, $\frac{5}{8}$" dia.: $3\frac{1}{2}$ ft.
Bailing wire, 16 gauge: 3 ft.
Brass ring, 10" dia.
Chain link: desired length
Dandelion diggers: 4
Grommets: green (4)
Swivel hook

Tools and General Supplies

Drill with $\frac{1}{4}$" bit
Grommet tool
Pipe cutter
Scissors
Sewing machine
Straight pins
Tracing paper
Wire cutters

Instructions

All seams are $\frac{1}{2}$" unless indicated otherwise.

1. From bailing wire, cut three pieces 25" long and eight pieces 4" long. Cut aluminum pipe into two 12" lengths and two 8" lengths. Note: A hardware store will cut the pipe for you if desired. Drill a hole through the top and bottom of each pipe.

2. Bundle 25" lengths of wire together. With heavy thread, bind together in center of wires. Separate wires to form a star shape and wrap each wire tightly. Stitch back through wrapping several times to secure. Bend wire down to brass ring and secure by twisting wire around with pliers.

3. Use 4"-long wires to connect dandelion diggers to pipes, forming legs. Paint legs with dark green spray enamel. Let dry completely.

4. Enlarge patterns on page 102. Place tracing paper over enlarged patterns and transfer all markings. Cut out individual patterns.

5. Referring to color pattern on page 102, trace pattern onto designated color of fabric. Cut out four crowns, and two each of A and B. Cut out remaining fabric pieces.

6. For eyes, sew A and B with right sides together leaving bottom open and easing B between dots on curved edge. Sew dart in B. Turn right side out and stuff with batting. From purple fabric, cut two 3" circles. Cover rounded buttons with purple circles. Sew black shank buttons in center of purple covered buttons. Stitch eyeballs to flat side of eyes.

7. With right sides together, sew the first three body panels together, stopping $\frac{1}{2}$" down from top. On right side of fabric, top-stitch down seams. Satin-stitch light green fabric into place on center panel for belly. Satin-stitch black mouth and black nose. Satin-stitch pink mouth onto bottom of black mouth.

8. Sew next three body panels together and sew one side to front panels. Top-stitch seams. Fold top under and top-stitch twice. Sew up last seam and top-stitch.

9. For crown, lightly trace points onto two pieces. Sew these two pieces, right sides together, at the side seams. Turn right side out. Sew other two pieces together in same manner. Slip second crown inside first crown with wrong sides together. Satin-stitch around bottom. Satin-stitch around points through both layers. Trim away excess fabric. Stitch crown to top of head.

10. Stitch eyes in place.

11. Slip body over wire frame. Pull tightly and pin excess under. Machine hem, skipping over wires. Attach two grommets to bottom edge of frog in front and a grommet on each side behind wires.

12. Attach legs through grommets with remaining 4" wires.

13. Attach swivel hook to wires inside of crown for hanging. Hang from desired length of chain link.

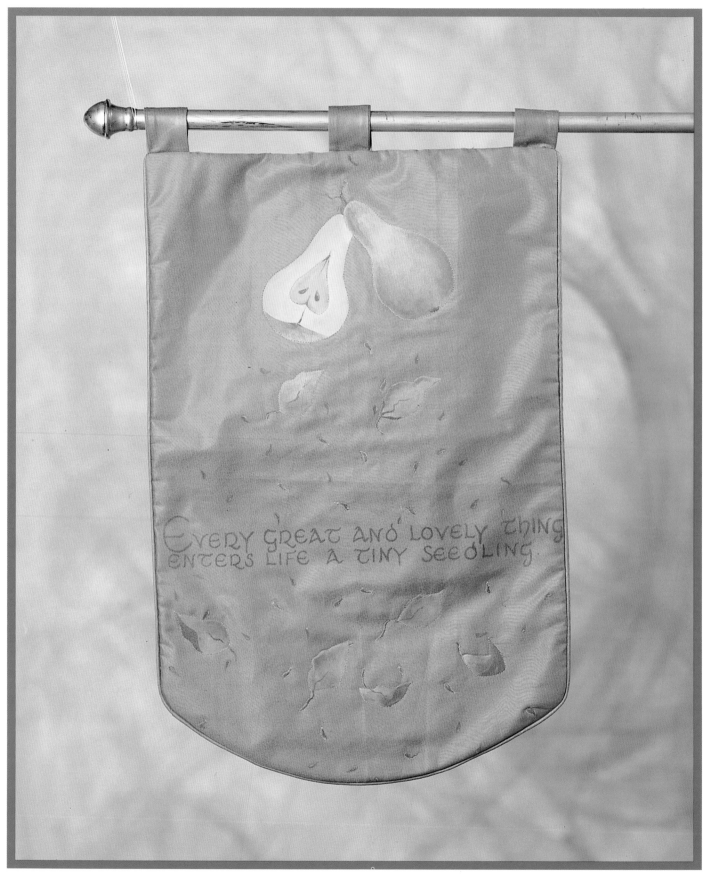

Pear Banner

Materials For Banner
Polished cotton fabrics: gold (5" square),
 peach (scrap), rust ($^2/_3$ yd.),
 tan (8" square)
Organza fabric: sheer ($^1/_2$ yd.)
Cotton cording: $1^2/_3$ yds.
Matching thread
Acrylic paints: autumn colors
Fleece batting: $^1/_2$ yd.
Fusible webbing: $^1/_4$ yd.

Tools and General Supplies
Iron and ironing board
Paintbrushes
Scissors
Sewing machine
Straight pins
Tracing paper
Transfer paper

Instructions
All seams are $^1/_2$" unless indicated otherwise.
Finished banner size is 13" x $19^1/_2$".

1. Enlarge pattern on page 103 and make template. Place tracing paper over enlarged template and trace. Cut out individual pieces. Trace patterns, except banner shape, onto fusible webbing. Trim around design, cutting just the general shape, not the exact pattern. Referring to color pattern on page 103, iron fusible patterns onto the wrong side of designated color of fabric. Cut out exact lines.

2. Using autumn colors of acrylic paint, shade and highlight pears and leaves.

3. Trace banner shape onto rust fabric and cut two. Cut enough bias strips from rust fabric to go around sides and bottom of banner. Cut three 4" x 3" strips for hanging tabs. Cut one banner shape from organza and one from fleece.

4. Arrange motifs on front of one rust banner piece and iron in place. Transfer lettering onto banner. Paint letters, seeds, and details with brown paint.

5. Place organza on top of banner front and fleece on back. Pin in place. Stitch around pears, leaves, and some seeds with a straight stitch.

6. Sew bias strips together. Place cording in the center of wrong side of bias strip. Fold fabric over and sew along edge of cording.

7. Fold each tab in half, long edge to long edge, right sides together. Sew side seam. Turn right side out and press.

8. Pin covered cording around front of banner, edge to edge. Actual cording should be pointing inward. Fold tabs in half and pin along top edge of banner with tabs pointing down. Place remaining rust banner piece on top of banner front with right sides together. Stitch around edges, leaving top open between two of the tabs. Clip curves and turn banner right side out. Whip-stitch opening closed.

Additional banner idea.
This Summer Tulips banner pattern is on page 116.

Apple Banner

Materials For Banner
Polished cotton fabrics: blue ($1/2$ yd.), lt.
    green ($1/8$ yd.), red ($1/8$ yd.), yellow ($1/2$ yd.)
Fleece batting: $1/2$ yd.
Thread: blue, lt. green, red, tan, yellow
Acrylic paints: beige, blue, brown, forest
    green, ivory, leaf green, lime green,
    maroon, dk. red, rose, yellow

Materials For Hanger
Cane: 84"
Small amount of raffia

Tools and General Supplies
Iron and ironing board
Paintbrushes
Pencil
Scissors
Sewing machine
Sewing needle
Straight pins
Tracing paper

Instructions
All seams are $1/2$" unless indicated otherwise.
Finished banner size is $16^{1}/_{2}$" x 22".

1. Enlarge pattern for banner shape on page 102 and make template. Trace banner shape and cut out top and bottom pattern. From blue fabric, cut two pieces for bottom half of banner. From yellow fabric, cut two pieces for top half of banner. Set aside.

2. Trace apple pattern from template and cut out. Trace six apples onto red fabric, four apples onto light green fabric, and four apples onto yellow fabric.

3. Highlight red apples with dark red, maroon, forest green, yellow, and ivory paint. Highlight yellow apples with yellow, lime green, beige, and ivory paint. Highlight light green apples with leaf green, rose, ivory, and forest green paint. Highlight stems with brown and ivory paint. Note: When highlighting, paintbrush should be fairly dry. After dipping paintbrush into paint, brush back and forth on a scrap of paper until most of paint is removed.

4. Transfer letter pattern from template to front of one yellow top piece. Paint letters blue. Let dry.

5. Sew painted yellow top of banner to one blue bottom of banner. For back of banner, sew remaining yellow and blue pieces together in same manner.

6. Cut out apples leaving a $1/4$" seam allowance. Clip curves in seam allowances and pin apples to blue section on front of banner, following pattern. Hand-sew apples in place turning edges under and using coordinating color thread.

7. From yellow fabric, cut two $1^{1}/_{2}$ x 7" strips. Bring long sides of each strip together and stitch seam along long edge. Turn and press, forming straps.

8. Cut banner shape from fleece batting. Place fleece onto work surface. Lay front of banner on top of fleece with right side up. Pin straps in place on front top of banner, allowing straps to point down. Place back of banner on top of front piece with right side down. Pin through all three layers. Sew around edges, leaving bottom open. Turn right side out.

9. Machine-quilt around apples with blue thread. Hand-tack bottom of banner closed.

10. For handle, cut cane into three 28" lengths. Holding all three together, wrap raffia around center 2". Tie off. Soak cane in water for 15 minutes. Remove and braid one side, curving downward as you go. Wrap raffia around end for 2". Tie off. Repeat for other side. Handle should form a half circle that will fit around top of banner. Stitch handle to top of banner with tan thread.

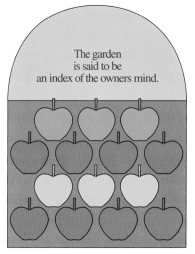

Additional color idea for the Apple Banner.

Coffee Cup Banner

Materials For Banner
Cotton fabrics: black (¹/₄ yd.), purple (¹/₂ yd.),
white (¹/₄ yd.), five assorted colors
(each 10" square)
Fleece batting: 1¹/₂ yds.
Fusible webbing: ¹/₃ yd.
Invisible thread
Heavy black thread
Black cording: 4 yds.

Materials For Hanger
Wooden dowel, 1¹/₂" dia.: 20"
Wooden finials to fit ends of dowel: 2
Acrylic paints: black, purple, white
Acrylic sealer
Double sided screws, ¹/₄" dia.: 1¹/₂" long (2)

Tools and General Supplies
Drill with ¹/₄" bit
Iron and ironing board
Paintbrushes
Pencil
Scissors
Sewing machine
Straight pins
Tracing paper

Instructions
All seams are ¹/₂" unless indicated otherwise.
Finished banner size is 5¹/₂" x 18".

1. Enlarge pattern on page 99. Transfer pattern to tracing paper and cut out.

2. Trace five coffee cup patterns onto fusible webbing. Trim around patterns, cutting the general shape, not the exact pattern. Iron fusible patterns onto the wrong side of each of the 10" fabric squares. Cut out the exact pattern from each fabric and set aside.

3. From purple fabric, cut one 11" x 46" piece and one 14" x 51" piece. From white fabric, cut sixteen 4" x 3¹/₂" pieces, six 4¹/₂ x 3" pieces, and one 9" x 5" piece. From black fabric, cut fourteen 4" x 3¹/₂" pieces, four 4¹/₂" x 3" pieces, four 4¹/₂" x 3¹/₂" pieces, and two 9" x 5" pieces.

4. Referring to color pattern on page 99, pin coffee cups to 11" x 46" purple fabric. Iron in place.

5. Using a decorative stitch or satin stitch, sew around coffee cups with heavy black thread. If hand sewing is preferred, a blanket stitch may be used.

6. To make side border, use eight 4" x 3½" white pieces and seven 4" x 3½" black pieces. Sew pieces together on the 3½" sides, alternating white and black. Repeat to make other side border. Place a border along one side of coffee cup banner with right sides together. Sew together. Fold border out and press. Repeat for other side.

7. For top border, use two 4½" x 3½" black pieces, two 4½" x 3" black pieces, and three 4½" x 3" white pieces. Starting and ending with a 4½" x 3½" black piece, sew pieces together on the 4½" sides alternating black and white. Repeat to make bottom border. Sew to top and bottom of banner in same manner as in step 6.

8. Press all edges under ½". Place banner right side down on work surface. Cut two pieces of fleece each 14" x 51". Place both layers of fleece onto wrong side of banner. Place 14" x 51" piece of purple fabric wrong side down on top of fleece. Pin all layers together.

9. Machine-quilt with invisible thread around coffee cups and borders. Fold edges under ½" and whip-stitch into place.

10. For hanging tabs, use one 9" x 5" white piece and two 9" x 5" black pieces. On each piece, bring long edges together and sew a seam. Turn and press. Make a loop with each tab and sew in place across top of banner. Turn edges of loops under and hem to back of banner.

11. To make hanging coffee cups, create a smaller coffee cup pattern. Trace pattern onto three different fabrics. Cut two from each fabric. Cut three patterns from fleece. Place a fleece pattern between two fabric patterns and hand-stitch a blanket stitch around edges with heavy black thread. Cut black cording into three different lengths. Attach a length of cording to each coffee cup and dangle from banner hanger.

12. For hanger, paint dowel purple and finials black and white. When dry, coat with acrylic sealer.

13. Drill holes into ends of dowels and into finials. Insert double-sided screws into each end of dowel. Slip banner onto dowel and screw finials into place.

Additional banner idea.
This "*riveting*" Welcome To Our Pad banner is to be wrapped around mailboxes; the pattern is on page 119.

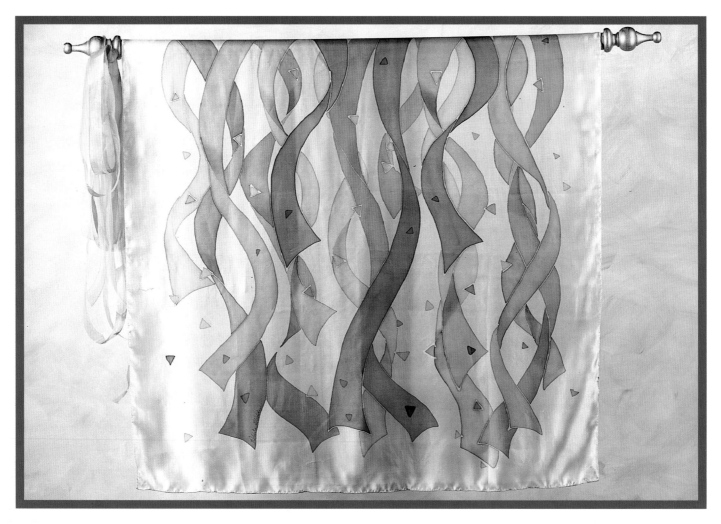

Painted Silk Banners

Materials For Banner
Silk satin: white (various sizes)
Fabric paint for silk: assorted colors
Water-soluble resist

Tools and General Supplies
Foam brushes
Iron and ironing board
Paintbrushes
Pencils: regular and charcoal
Scissors
Sewing machine
Straight pins
Stretcher bars
Tracing paper

Instructions
Instructions for painting on these silk banners can be found on page 19; the patterns are on page 109. The following are a few additional ideas:

- Scarves purchased on trips may be used as memory banners.

- Try hanging different holiday banners to celebrate the seasons.

- Add real ribbons, jewels, trims or other extra adornments to these painted banners.

- Hang the banners from staircases, vaulted ceilings—just about anywhere.

- Make small theme scarves such as fruits, vegetables or recipes to hang in the kitchen or scarves with floral or seashell designs to hang in the bathroom.

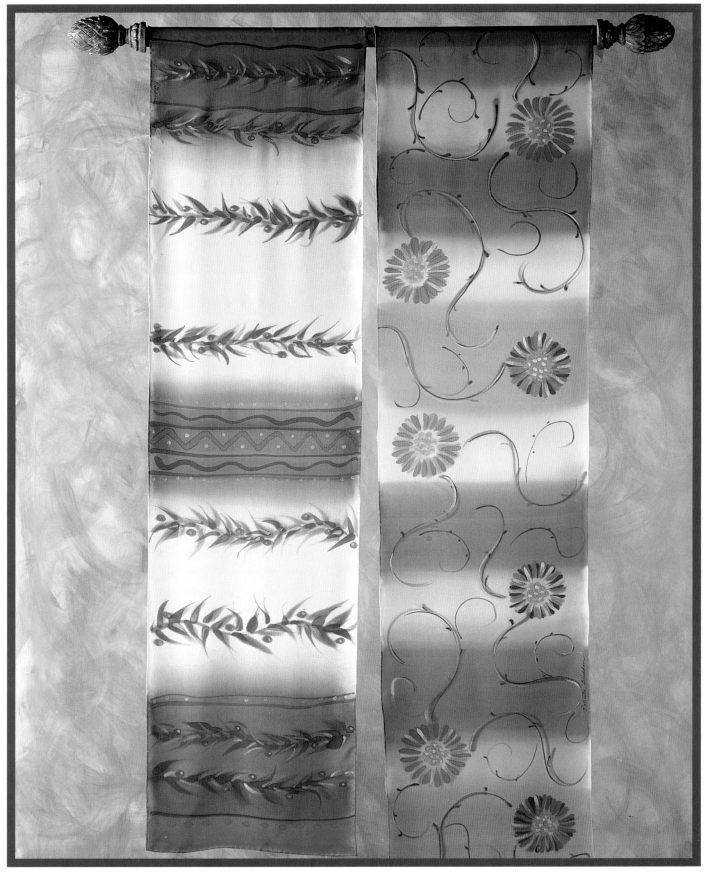

Log Cabin Banner

Materials For Banner

Coarse-weave fabrics: green (¹/₄ yd.),
 tan (¹/₂ yd.)
Moiré fabric: dk. green (2" x 6"),
 lt. green (4" x 12")
Braided trim, ³/₈": 6"
Iridescent ribbon, 1": brown (5¹/₂")
Metallic ribbon, 1": copper (3")
Satin ribbon, ⁵/₈": brown (3¹/₂ yds.)
Satin ribbon, 1¹/₂": white (7")
Wired ribbon, 1": ombré green (28")
Wired ribbon, 1¹/₂": black (¹/₂ yd.)
Thread: black, brown, dk. green, invisible,
 iridescent gold, yellow
Small bead: brown
Fusible interfacing: ¹/₂ yd.
Fusible webbing: 6" x 12"

Materials For Hanger

Stick: 18"

Tools and General Supplies

Iron and ironing board
Pencil
Scissors
Sewing machine
Sewing needle
Straight pins
Tracing paper

Instructions

All seams are ¹/₂" unless indicated otherwise.
Finished banner size is 15¹/₂" x 20¹/₂".

1. Trace patterns for trees, stars, chimney, and bird from page 108. Cut out traced patterns.

2. Trace patterns (except chimney) onto fusible webbing. Trim around patterns, cutting just the general shape, not the exact pattern. Using the color pattern on page 108 as a guide, iron fusible patterns onto the wrong side of designated color of fabric or ribbon.

3. Cut out the exact patterns from materials. Set aside. From tan fabric, cut two 16" x 20¹/₂" pieces. From fusible interfacing, cut a 16" 20¹/₂" piece. Fuse interfacing to wrong side of one of the tan pieces, forming banner front.

4. From brown satin ribbon, cut nine strips, each 6" long. Fold ends under ¹/₄" and press. Place banner front vertically on work surface. Starting 5" in from left side and 4" up from bottom, place one brown strip horizontally and pin in place. Continue placing strips up the banner ¹/₄" apart to form logs.

5. Holding wire at both ends, gather black wired ribbon to measure 9". Cut a piece of fusible interfacing the same shape. Fuse to back of black ribbon to hold the gathered shape. Place chimney pattern over black ribbon and cut shape. Pin chimney in place. Satin-stitch logs and chimney in place with matching thread.

6. Using metallic copper ribbon for the door, sew onto front of cabin with a straight stitch and invisible thread. Sew small bead in place for doorknob.

7. Using iridescent brown ribbon for roof, fold top corners back and press. Sew onto top log with a straight stitch and invisible thread.

8. Pin trees in desired position. Cut brown braided trim into three lengths for tree trunks. Tuck top of trunk under tree and tack bottom of trunk to banner. Iron trees in place. Satin-stitch around trees with matching thread.

9. Iron crow and stars in place. Satin-stitch around crow with black thread. Satin-stitch crow's legs with yellow thread. Satin-stitch around stars with gold iridescent thread.

10. Gather one edge of green ombré ribbon to desired length. Placing gathered edge down, pin along bottom of cabin for grass. Sew in place with straight stitches and invisible thread.

11. Place other tan piece on back of banner and stitch around sides.

12. Cut green fabric into two pieces 4" x 16", and two pieces 4" x 20¹/₂". On each strip, fold long ends into the center and press. Fold in half and press. Pin the 16" strips in place along top and bottom of banner. Pin the 20¹/₂" strips in place along the sides of banner. Stitch border in place.

13. From brown satin ribbon, cut six 10" lengths. Fold each piece in half. Sew two at each position across top of banner for hangers. Insert stick through hangers.

Stamped Sunflowers

Materials For Banner

Muslin fabric: natural (1¼ yds.)

Matching thread

Acrylic paints: blue-gray, brown, dk. cream, lt. cream, gray-green, rust, white, lt. yellow, med. yellow

Glaze paints: brown, green, neutral, rust, yellow, yellow-green

Textile medium

Dense craft foam (or purchased sunflower decorator foam stamping block)

Materials For Hanger

Wooden dowel: 30"

Wooden beads: to fit ends of dowel

Optional: Rabbit Banner Holder (instructions on page 88)

Tools and General Supplies

Craft knife

Paintbrushes

Pencil

Scissors

Sewing machine

Sponge

Tracing paper

Transfer paper

Instructions

All seams are ½" unless indicated otherwise.
Finished banner size is 21½" x 42½".

1. Cut muslin into two 22½" x 45" pieces.

2. Enlarge patterns for houses and stars on page 107. Place tracing paper over enlarged patterns and transfer all markings. Place patterns in desired position on the right side of one of the muslin pieces. Insert transfer paper between pattern and muslin and lightly trace designs.

3. Mix acrylic paints with textile medium following manufacturer's instructions. Thinning the paint with a little water allows the paint to be applied more smoothly to the fabric. However, using thinned paint around the pattern edges could cause bleeding. Paint bottom of houses dark cream. Highlight with light cream. Paint roofs with blue-gray. Highlight by sponging on gray-green and white paints. Paint windows with blue-gray. Paint chimneys rust and doors brown. Paint stars medium yellow and highlight with rust and light yellow.

4. With pencil, lightly draw a path from right bottom of house down to left center bottom of banner. Sponge along path with dark cream and light cream. Use yellow-green and yellow glaze paints to highlight path. Sponge paint around top of path with green and yellow glazes, forming bushes.

5. Trace sunflower petals and leaves onto tracing paper and cut out. Place motifs onto foam and trace. With craft knife, cut motifs from foam. Cut any details into foam such as veins or seeds. Note: A purchased sunflower decorator block may be used, eliminating this step.

6. Apply glazes to foam stamps referring to instructions page 19. Stamp sunflowers and leaves randomly across bottom of banner, blending as desired. Paint in flower centers.

7. When completely dry, place both muslin pieces right sides together. Sew around sides and bottom. Turn right side out and hem top edge. Turn top edge back another 1½" and hem to form a casing.

8. Paint wooden dowel as desired. Slip banner onto dowel.

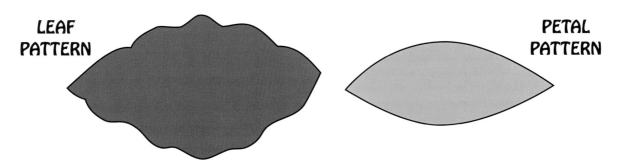

LEAF PATTERN

PETAL PATTERN

Rabbit Banner Holder

Materials For Hanger

Acrylic paints: black, brown, cream,
   dk. green, pink, tan
Wood primer
Wood deck sealer
Buttons: black (5)
Wooden board: $5/8$" x 4' x 6'
Nails
Wood screws, $1^1/4$": 3
Large eye screws: 4
Rebar: 4'

Tools and General Supplies

Drill with 1" hole saw bit
Hammer
Pencil
Paintbrushes
Saw
Screwdriver
Tracing paper

Instructions

1. Enlarge rabbit pattern. Place a large sheet of tracing paper over pattern and transfer all markings. Trace rabbit piece and arm piece onto wooden board and Cut out pieces with saw.

2. From wooden board, cut two $22^1/4$" x $3^1/4$" pieces for long sides, two 15" x $3^1/4$" pieces for short sides, and one 24" x 15" piece for base. In center of base, cut a 1" x 4" slit. Nail side pieces together to form a frame. Place base on top of frame and nail down. Drill a 1" hole just above the center of slit.

3. Paint all wood with wood primer. Paint base tan. With pencil, transfer pattern detail onto rabbit and arm and paint as desired. When all paint has dried, apply wood deck sealer.

4. Screw arm into place on rabbit. Glue buttons onto jacket. Screw two eye screws onto back center of rabbit, one 36" up from bottom and one 10" higher. Screw remaining two eye screws into protruding part of rabbit's arm. These screws should be angled so that when a dowel (banner holder) is placed through them, the banner will look as though the rabbit is holding it.

5. Place rabbit into slit in base. Slip rebar down through eye screws and into hole in base.

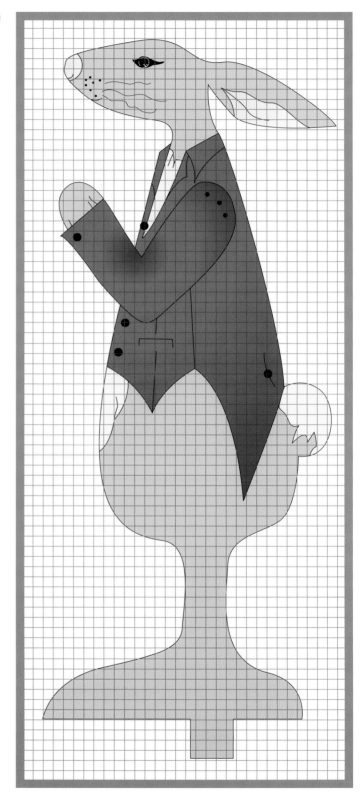

RABBIT PATTERN

Welcome Home
Birdhouses

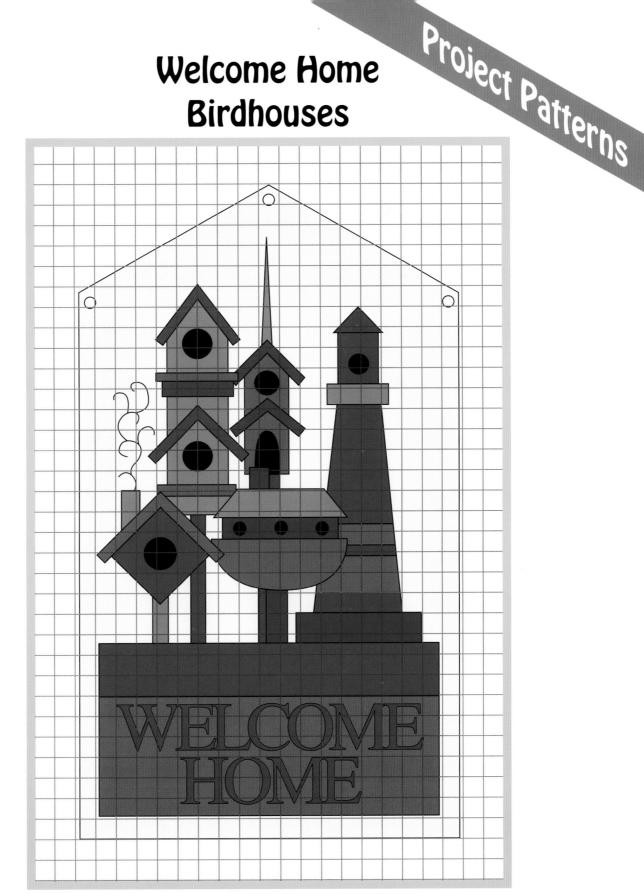

Welcome Home Birdhouses banner instructions on page 45.

Long Live The Queen

Long Live the Queen banner instructions on page 23.

Best Witches

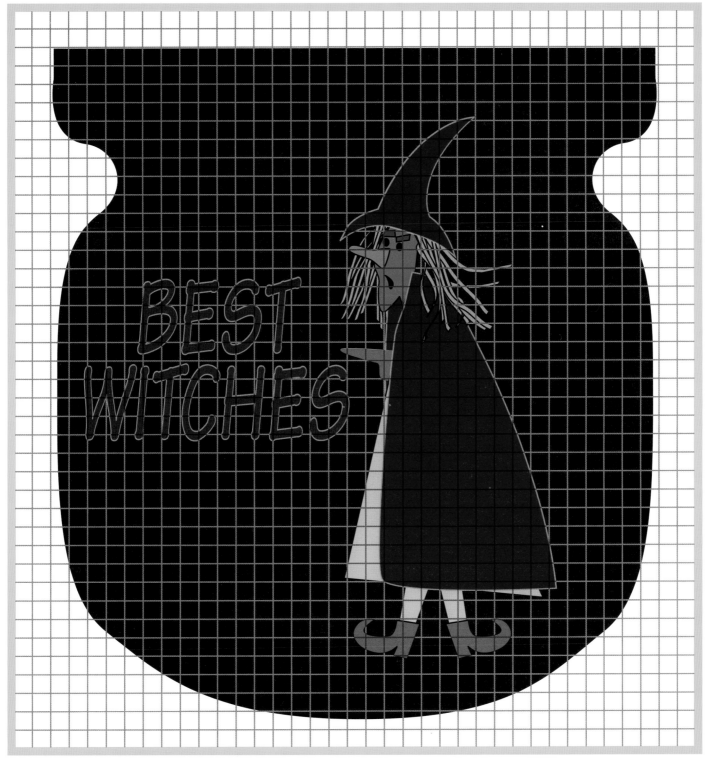

Best Witches banner instructions on page 25.

Noah's Ark

Noah's Ark banner instructions on page 47.

Sun Banner

Sun Banner instructions on page 53.

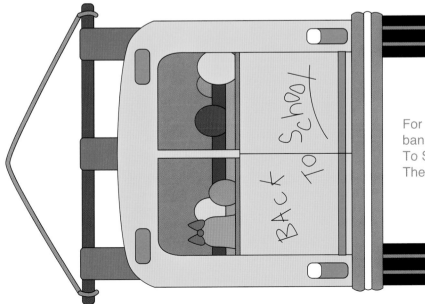

For an additional seasonal banner idea, try this Back To School Bus banner. The pattern is on page 122.

Autumn Leaves Banner

Autumn Leaves Banner instructions on page 31.

Winter Banners

Winter Banners instructions on page 32-35.

Harvest Angel Banner

Harvest Angel Banner instructions on page 65.

Keep On Trikin'

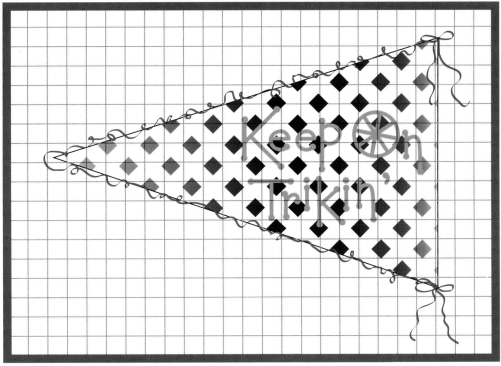

Keep On Trikin' banner instructions on page 61.

Biker Banner

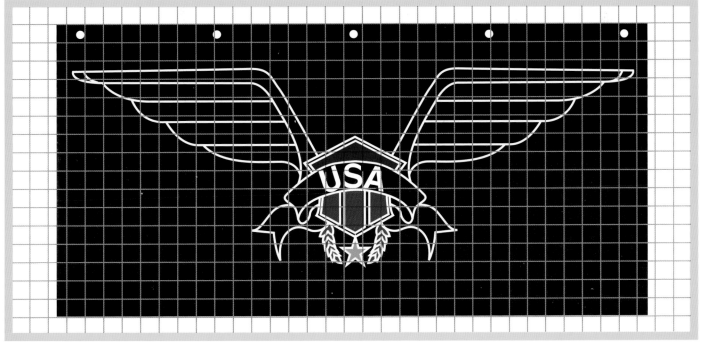

Biker Banner instructions on page 59.

Fishing Banner

Fishing Banner instructions on page 55.

For an additional banner to hang from a boat, try this Skull & Cross Bones banner. The pattern is on page 123.

RV Banner

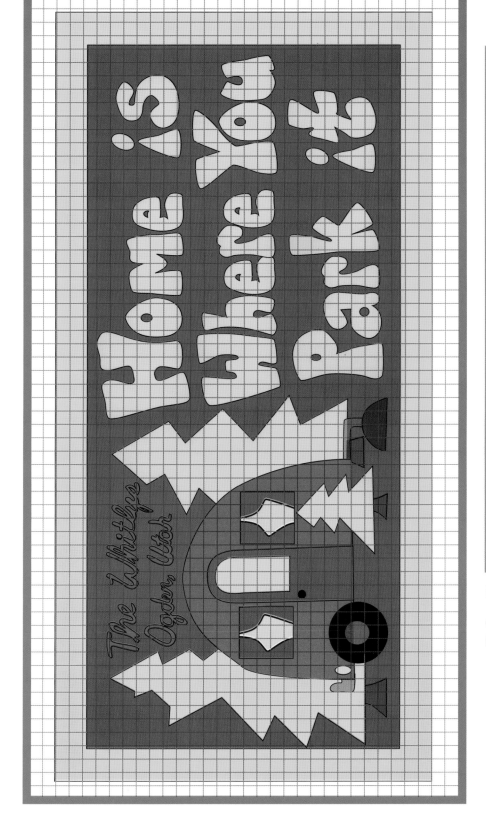

Coffee Cup Banner

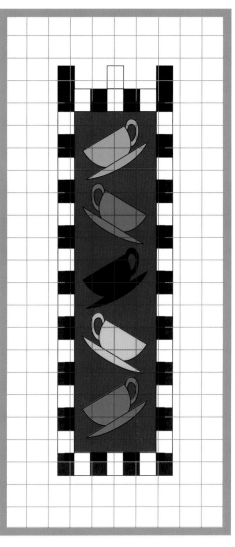

RV Banner instructions on page 58.

Coffee Cup Banner instructions on page 80.

Oak Leaves & Acorns

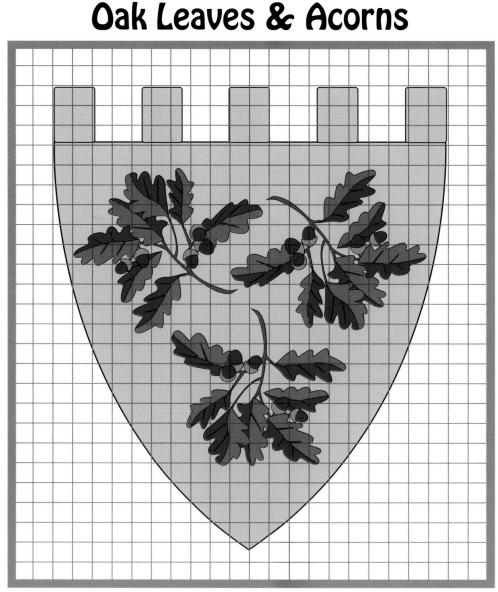

Oak Leaves & Acorns banner instructions on page 27.

For additional fall banners try this Happy Haunting banner. The pattern is on page 123.

Northwoods Cabin Banner

Northwoods Cabin Banner instructions on page 62.

Apple Banner

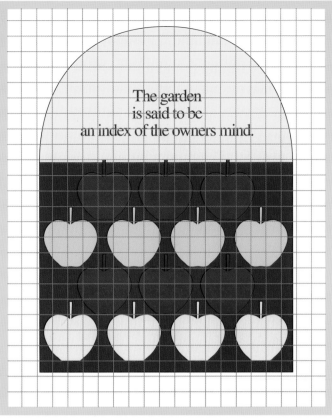

Apple Banner instructions on page 79.

Frog Banner

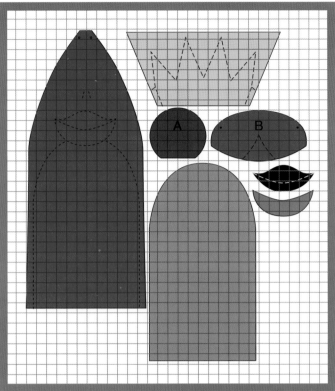

Frog Banner instructions on page 75.

Flannel Shirt

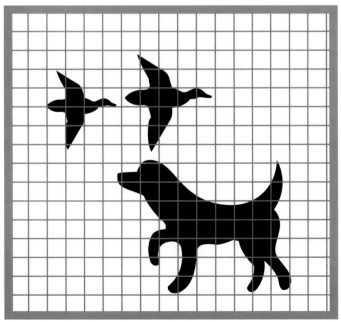

Flannel Shirt banner instructions on page 67.

Clubhouse Banner

Clubhouse Banner instructions on page 65.

Pear Banner

Pear Banner instructions on page 77.

Teatime Cat Banner

Teatime Cat Banner instructions on page 73.

Butterfly Banner

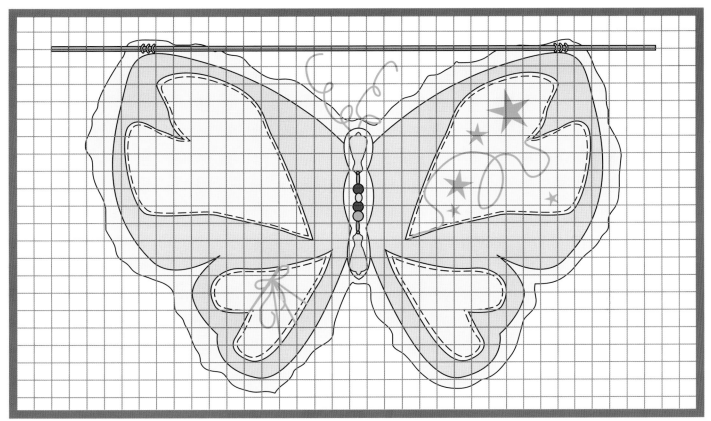

Angel's Sing

Butterfly Banner instructions on page 51.

Angel's Sing banner instructions on page 29.

Birds of a Feather

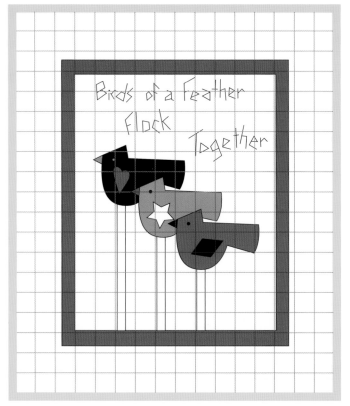

Everybody Needs Their Spot

Garden Banner

Birds of a Feather banner instructions on page 71.

Everybody Needs Their Spot banner instructions on page 68.

Garden Banner instructions on page 49.

Stamped Sunflowers

Stamped Sunflowers banner instructions on page 87.

Log Cabin Banner

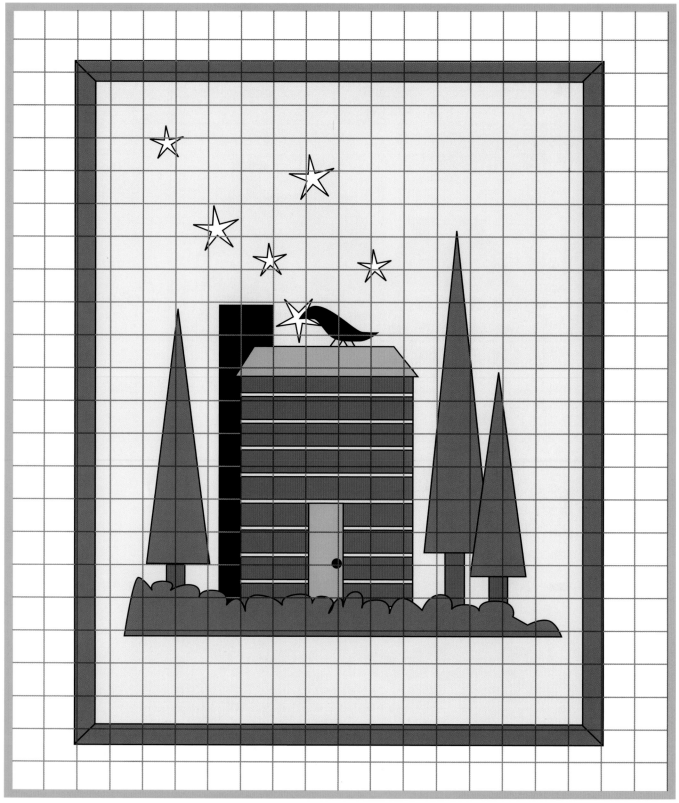

Log Cabin Banner instructions on page 85.

Painted Silk Banners

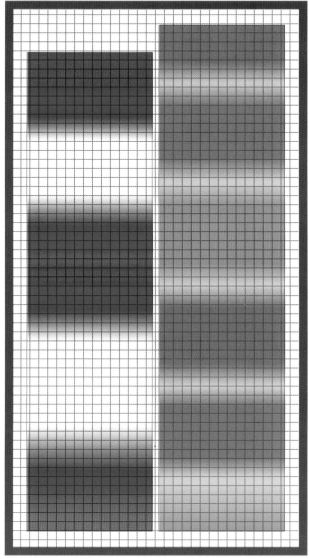

Painted Silk Banner instructions on pages 19 & 82.

Holiday Home Quilt

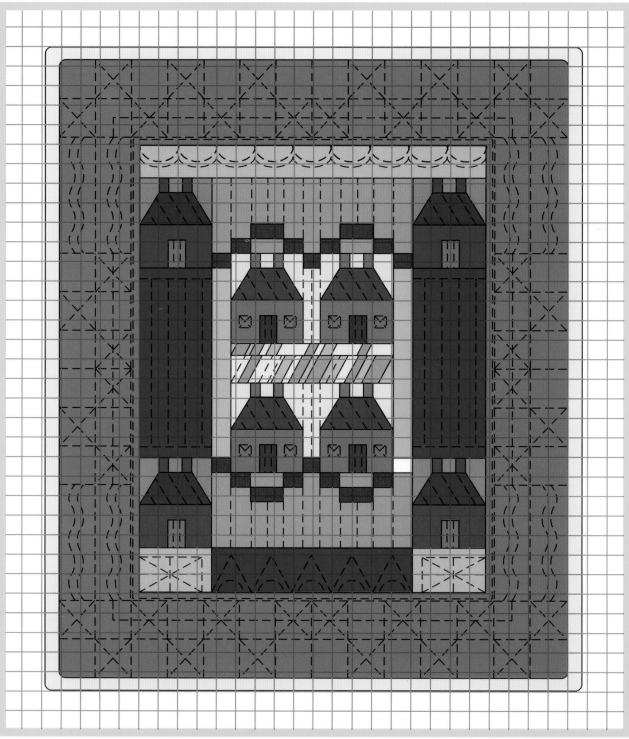

Holiday Home Quilt banner photo on page 2.

This banner can be made using desired techniques—piece or appliqué the banner for a more difficult project or paint it for an easier project. The finished banner size is 28" x 33". An experienced quilter may wish to quilt this project; others attempting to quilt this design should consult specialty books for detailed instructions.

Let It Snow banner pattern on page 124.

Ho Ho Ho Stocking banner pattern on page 125.

Peace Dove banner pattern on page 125.

Valentine Heart

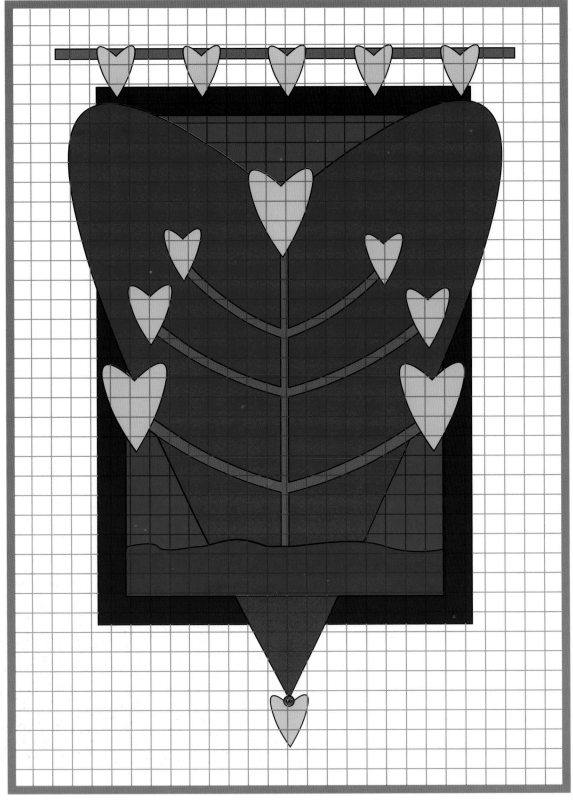

Valentine Heart banner drawing on inside front cover.

112

Spring Duck

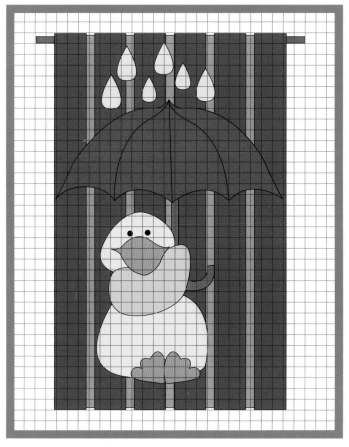

Congratulations

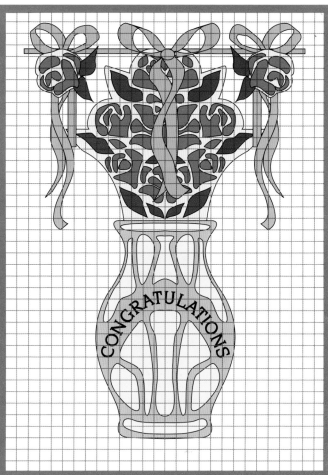

Patchwork Heart

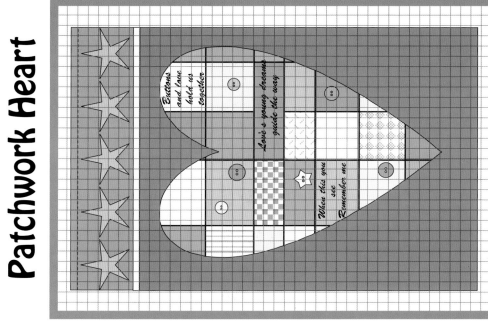

Spring Duck banner drawing on page 71.

Congratulations banner drawing on page 9.

Patchwork Heart banner drawing on page 3.

Spring Blossoms

Blossom by blossom the spring begins...

Spring Blossoms banner drawing on page 1.

St. Patrick's Day Cats

Miracles happen to those who believe in them.

St. Patrick's Day Cats banner drawing on page 69.

Welcome Little One

welcome little one

Welcome Little Ones banner drawing on page 45.

Easter Lilies

Easter Lilies banner drawing on inside front cover.

Summer Tulips

A Day At The Beach

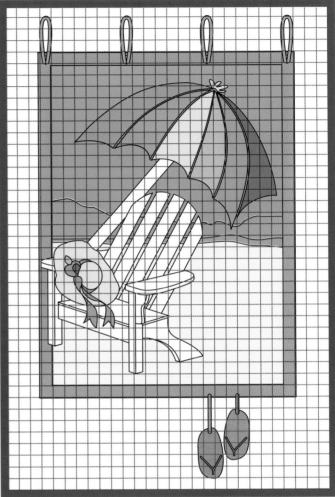

Graduation Banner

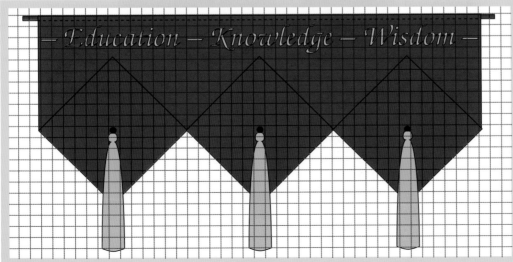

Summer Tulips banner
drawing on page 77.

A Day At The Beach banner
drawing on page 53.

Graduation banner drawing
on page 4.

Vivid Butterfly

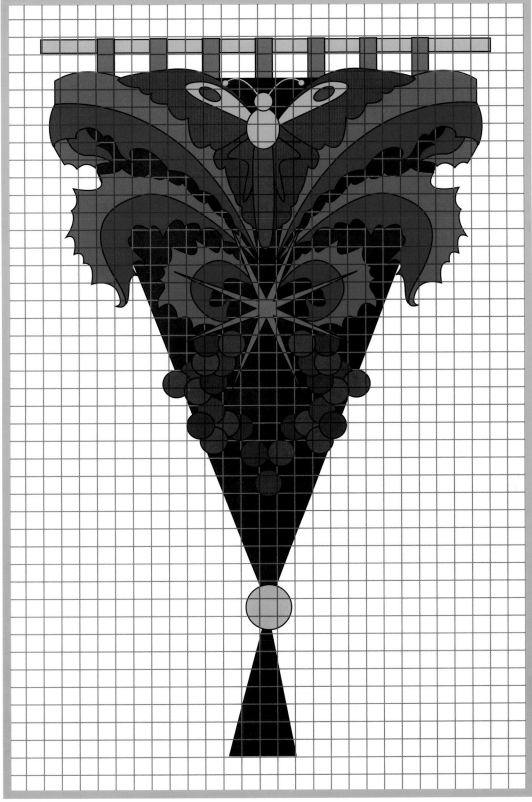

Vivid Butterfly banner drawing on page 5.

Earth Day Banner

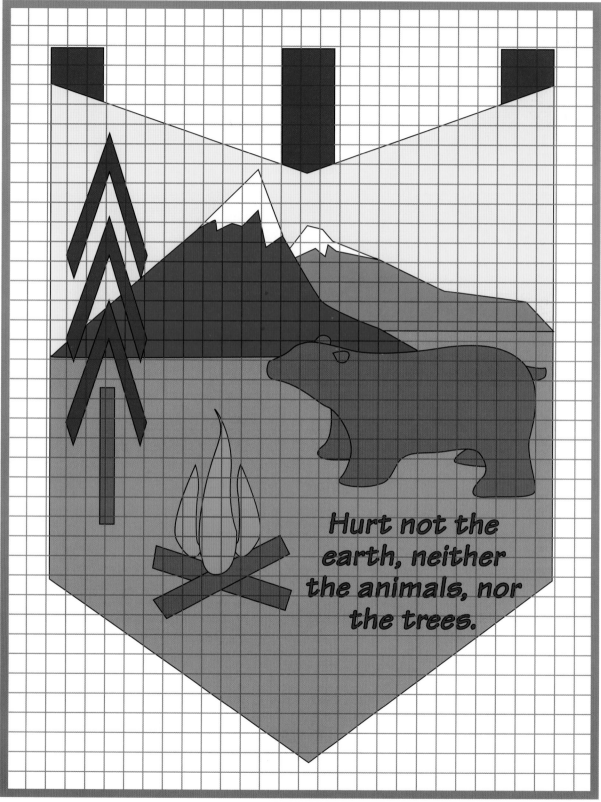

Hurt not the earth, neither the animals, nor the trees.

Earth Day banner drawing on page 27.

Family Banner

Welcome To Our Pad

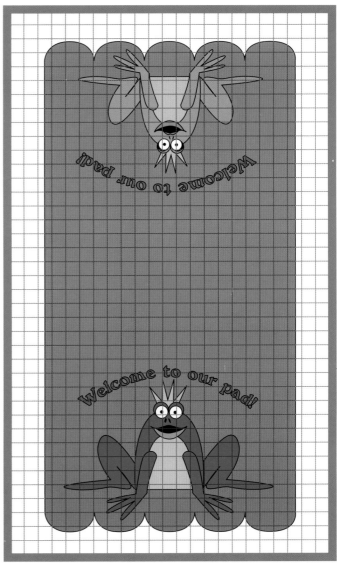

Alphabet

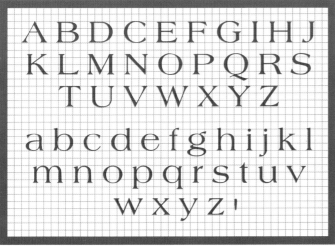

Family banner drawing on page 31. Use the provided alphabet, or the any other desired alphabet, to personalize banner.

Welcome To Our Pad banner drawing on page 81. Wrap completed banner around top of mailbox. Secure bottom edges around bottom of mailbox with heavy-duty thread.

Hats Off To Dad

Hats Off To Dad banner drawing on page 55.

Attach real fishing lures, decorative key chains, or trinkets to dangle from bottom of banner.

Wild & Crazy Mom

Wild & Crazy Mom banner drawing on page 23.

Use different colors of ric-rac for hair. For dimensional hair try different colors of pipe cleaners coiled around a pencil and tacked onto banner.

Good To Eat

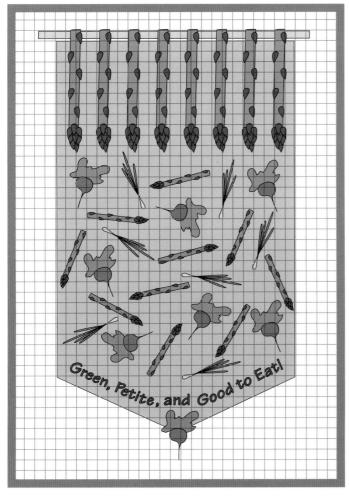

Flowers & Laughter Chair

Queen of the Road

Good To Eat banner drawing on page 49.

Flowers & Laughter Chair banner drawing on page 18.

Queen of the Road banner drawing on page 61.

Back To School Bus

Back To School Bus banner drawing on page 93.

Happy Haunting

Happy Haunting banner drawing on page 100.

Skull & Cross Bones

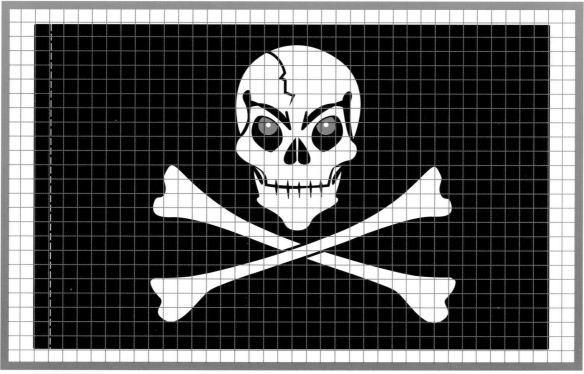

Skull & Cross Bones banner drawing on page 98.

Innocent Pie-stander

Just an   Innocent   Pie-stander

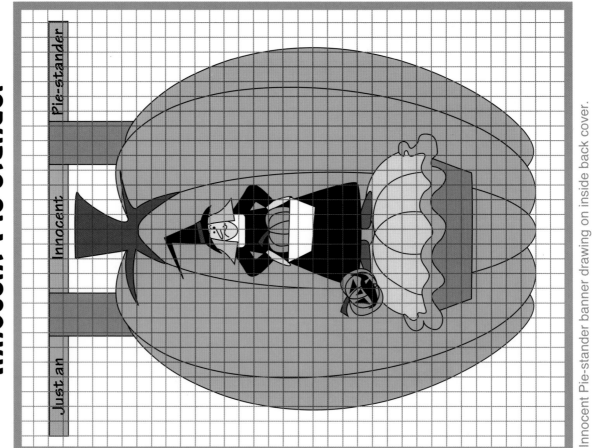

Innocent Pie-stander banner drawing on inside back cover.

Let It Snow

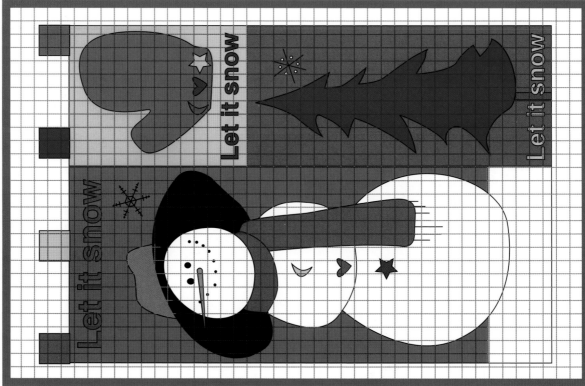

Let It Snow banner drawing on page 111.

METRIC EQUIVALENCE CHART

MM-Millimetres   CM-Centimetres

INCHES TO MILLIMETRES AND CENTIMETRES

INCHES	MM	CM	INCHES	CM	INCHES	CM
⅛	3	0.3	9	22.9	30	76.2
¼	6	0.6	10	25.4	31	78.7
½	13	1.3	12	30.5	33	83.8
⅝	16	1.6	13	33.0	34	86.4
¾	19	1.9	14	35.6	35	88.9
⅞	22	2.2	15	38.1	36	91.4
1	25	2.5	16	40.6	37	94.0
1¼	32	3.2	17	43.2	38	96.5
1½	38	3.8	18	45.7	39	99.1
1¾	44	4.4	19	48.3	40	101.6
2	51	5.1	20	50.8	41	104.1
2½	64	6.4	21	53.3	42	106.7
3	76	7.6	22	55.9	43	109.2
3½	89	8.9	23	58.4	44	111.8
4	102	10.2	24	61.0	45	114.3
4½	114	11.4	25	63.5	46	116.8
5	127	12.7	26	66.0	47	119.4
6	152	15.2	27	68.6	48	121.9
7	178	17.8	28	71.1	49	124.5
8	203	20.3	29	73.7	50	127.0

YARDS TO METRES

YARDS	METRES	YARDS	METRES	YARDS	METRES	YARDS	METRES	YARDS	METRES
⅛	0.11	2⅛	1.94	4⅛	3.77	6⅛	5.60	8⅛	7.43
¼	0.23	2¼	2.06	4¼	3.89	6¼	5.72	8¼	7.54
⅜	0.34	2⅜	2.17	4⅜	4.00	6⅜	5.83	8⅜	7.66
½	0.46	2½	2.29	4½	4.11	6½	5.94	8½	7.77
⅝	0.57	2⅝	2.40	4⅝	4.23	6⅝	6.06	8⅝	7.89
¾	0.69	2¾	2.51	4¾	4.34	6¾	6.17	8¾	8.00
⅞	0.80	2⅞	2.63	4⅞	4.46	6⅞	6.29	8⅞	8.12
1	0.91	3	2.74	5	4.57	7	6.40	9	8.23
1⅛	1.03	3⅛	2.86	5⅛	4.69	7⅛	6.52	9⅛	8.34
1¼	1.14	3¼	2.97	5¼	4.80	7¼	6.63	9¼	8.46
1⅜	1.26	3⅜	3.09	5⅜	4.91	7⅜	6.74	9⅜	8.57
1½	1.37	3½	3.20	5½	5.03	7½	6.86	9½	8.69
1⅝	1.49	3⅝	3.31	5⅝	5.14	7⅝	6.97	9⅝	8.80
1¾	1.60	3¾	3.43	5¾	5.26	7¾	7.09	9¾	8.92
1⅞	1.71	3⅞	3.54	5⅞	5.37	7⅞	7.20	9⅞	9.03
2	1.83	4	3.66	6	5.49	8	7.32	10	9.14

Index

Happy New Year Jester banner pattern on page 126.

Ho Ho Ho Stocking

To All A Good Night

Peace On Earth

Ho Ho Ho Stocking banner drawing on page 111.

To All A Good Night banner drawing on inside back cover.

Peace On Earth banner drawing on page 111.

Happy New Year Jester

Happy New Year Jester banner drawing on page 128.